Landrace Gardening

Food Security
through Biodiversity
and Promiscuous Pollination

What People Are Saying About Landrace Gardening

"Awesome to see this process beginning to work in just one year." Josh Jamison, HEART Village

"Severe weather patterns impact our crops and gardens, but Joseph's book shows us, in simple terms, how to breed resilience into our favorite food plants. In these pages, he explains the steps for becoming your own seed breeder and highlights the easiest crops to begin with. His brilliant breeding work, briefly but vividly captured here, inspires us to try our hand at it, and to have loving patience for what will unfold." Merlla McLaughlin, editor

"Joseph's book is an eye-opener to a novice seed saver like myself. My growing conditions are not as extreme as Joseph's, but we do have a very short growing season. He has inspired me to start trying to produce my own landrace crops." Megan Palmer

"Inspiring. Empowering. VERY important work." Stephanie Genus

"Octavia E. Butler's Earthseed, John Twelve Hawks' Traveler Series, and Orson Scott-Card's Ender Quintet have delivered us to Joseph's fertile gateway. Not a gateway 'drug,' but yes a door of perception. In this book, Joseph removes from our lexicon Instant, Lite, Diet, Recommended Daily Allowance, Modern, Heirloom, Open Pollinated, Hybrid with just one shattering word: Promiscuous. Under the same condition he was once gifted a guitar, Joseph offers us Abundance for as long as we keep learning to play within it." Heron Breen, Fedco Seeds

Landrace Gardening

Food Security
through Biodiversity
and Promiscuous Pollination

Joseph Lofthouse
Landrace Seedkeeper

Publisher's Cataloging-in-Publication Data
(Prepared by The Donohue Group, Inc.)

Names: Lofthouse, Joseph, author.
Title: Landrace gardening: food security through biodiversity and
    promiscuous pollination / Joseph Lofthouse, landrace seedkeeper.
Description: First edition. | Paradise, Utah, United States of America:
    Father of Peace Ministry, 2021. | Includes index.
Identifiers: ISBN 9780578245652 (paperback)
Subjects: LCSH: Organic gardening. | Subsistence farming. | Plant
    breeding. | Seeds—Harvesting. | Pollination. | Heirloom varieties
    (Plants)
Classification: LCC SB454.3.L36 L64 2021 | DDC 635.04—dc23

Edited by: Merlla McLaughlin

Graphics and layout were designed using open source software and fonts: GIMP, LibreOffice, EB Garamond font family.

Published by Father of Peace Ministry,
Paradise, Utah, United States of America

Contact the author or join his mailing list at https://Lofthouse.com
Please post reviews to your favorite shopping or social media sites.

This book available as:

Description;	ISBN
Paperback, premium color photos;	9780578245652
Hardcover, premium color photos;	9781737325000
Large print, hardcover, text only;	9781737325017
Student edition, paperback, black/white;	9781737325093
Chinese, paperback, standard color	9781737325031

Dedicated to the millions
of freelance seed-keepers who
spent tens of thousands of years
domesticating the species
that I now grow.

Glossary

Common bean: I often include "common" when talking about beans to specify the species Phaseolus vulgaris, which are beans like pinto, kidney, and great northern.

Cross-pollination: Occurs when a mother plant receives pollen from a plant that is not closely related.

Heirloom: A variety that has undergone open pollinated inbreeding for more than 50 years.

Parts of a flower

Inbreeding depression: Describes the loss of vigor that occurs when plants become highly inbred.

Inter-pollination: A synonym for cross-pollination.

Landrace: A locally-adapted, genetically-diverse, promiscuously-pollinating food crop. Landraces are intimately connected to the land, ecosystem, farmer, and community. Landraces offer food security through their ability to adapt to changing conditions.

Male sterile: A plant that does not produce pollen. The anthers are often missing or deformed. Male flowers may be entirely absent.

Open pollination: The practice of isolating and inbreeding plant varieties, to keep them pure. This ensures that they remain stable from year to year. The intense inbreeding limits the ability of open-pollinated crops to adapt to changes in growing conditions.

Phenotype: The observed or measured traits of a plant or animal. Phenotype is influenced by genetic makeup and environmental conditions.

Promiscuous pollination: The practice of encouraging cross-pollination. The goals of seed saving are genetic diversity and local adaptation, not stability of phenotype.

Selfing: Describes a plant or population that is self-pollinating.

Self-incompatible: Describes a plant that is not capable of self-pollinating. Self-incompatible plants are 100% outcrossing.

Winnowing: Using wind to separate seeds from chaff.

Table of Contents

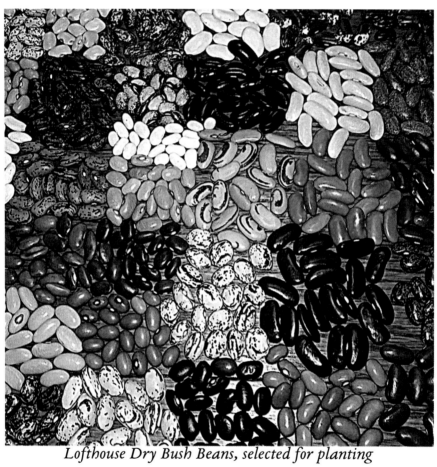

Lofthouse Dry Bush Beans, selected for planting

Acknowledgments

Father Sun and Mother Gaia provide the living and inorganic systems upon which my life and plant breeding efforts depend. I feel grateful for the processes that created life, and endowed me with the intellectual and emotional capacity to live in conscious relationships with the plants, animals, and natural world.

I am grateful to the microbes, endophytes, fungi, bacteria, and viruses that are vital to my health, and that of the plants and animals on my farm.

Millions of seed savers, who didn't read or write, domesticated the plants that I grow. I acknowledge that my plant breeding is minor rearranging of the preexisting genetics.

My parents and grandparents taught me to farm and to respect the natural world and my place in it. I thank my ancestors, who lived close to the land and natural cycles of life, growth, and death. I appreciate that my family has chosen to eat food grown in our gardens, harvested from the nearby wildlands, or produced locally by organic farmers.

I am grateful to the land stewards who allowed me to plant: The Bremmer, Graham, Stuart, MacAtee, and Delgado families; my parents; my sisters Amy and Cheryl; and my brother Steve.

Alan Bishop, founder of the Homegrown Goodness plant breeding forum, introduced me to the idea of landrace gardening. I appreciate each member of the forum. They helped me to better understand landrace plant breeding and traditional agricultural methods.

Alan Kapuler's ideas about plant breeding informed many of the early discussions on the forum.

Ken Ottinger of the Long Island Seed Project inspired me to grow landrace crops, and provided many of my original varieties.

Raoul Robinson wrote *Return to Resistance: Breeding Crops to Reduce Pesticide Dependence*. It is tremendously valuable to me. Due to its teachings, I welcome pests and diseases as treasured collaborators, not as fear-inducing enemies.

Carol Deppe wrote *Breed Your Own Vegetable Varieties: The Gardener's and Farmer's Guide to Plant Breeding and Seed Saving*. It introduced me to book-learning about plant breeding and seed saving. Its recommendations were instrumental in my early plant breeding efforts. The second edition's appendix of plant species has consistently been my most useful reference tool.

She took a personal interest in my work. I value her insights about my projects.

Open Source Seed Initiative and its governing board, staff, and donors fund the Open Source Plant Breeding Forum, and travel expenses to get me to conferences. I appreciate each member of the forum for sharing their ideas and breeding projects, and for helping me to refine my thinking and understanding.

Bill McDorman and Rocky Mountain Seed Alliance, and its board of directors and staff got me off the farm for the first time, and many times since. They encouraged me to grow into the role of seed elder.

Dan Barber, Matthew Goldfarb, Michael Mazourek, Myra Manning, and Petra Page-Mann of Blue Hill at Stone Barns, Row 7 Seeds, and/or Fruition Seeds offered support, tutelage, and encouragement, especially regarding the promiscuous tomato project. More generally, they helped me grow into a more well-rounded and playful farmer and human.

Experimental Farm Network is distributing my seeds, thus freeing my time for plant breeding, teaching, travel, and writing. Baker Creek Heirloom Seeds made a substantial donation to help with my work. This book wouldn't exist without the support of these two companies and their customers.

The Beautifully Promiscuous and Tasty Tomato Project benefited from an unknown angel that sent me seeds of wild tomato species. (I'm sorry that I misplaced your name. If you read this, I'd love to hear from you.)

I appreciate the people who grow the landrace varieties that I have come to love, especially the people that send grow reports. It brings joy to a plant breeder to receive letters that say things like: "A cantaloupe matured in my garden for the first time." "They taste amazing!" The grow reports motivate me to grow enough excess seed to share.

Dawn Andersson, Vivi Logan, Jennifer Willis, and Gregg Batt provided photos. Sage Austin mentored me on photo design.

This book improved with feedback from people who reviewed prepublication editions: Steve Lowe, Dave Blanchard, Megan Palmer, Kari Durfee, Bernd Bosma, Eleni Wilding, Karin Kee, Claire D'Gaia, Yehonathan Neta, Susan Searless, and Amy Simmons.

Jason Padvorac's prepublication review was particularly useful in helping me to more fully incorporate my heart-song into the book.

Dawn Andersson, Kay Everts, Greg Martin, and David Languignon helped with prepublication expenses.

Merlla McLaughlin edited the book with respect for my unique voice and dialect. Her early guidance shaped the organization and flow of the book. Later editing helped me express my heart-song using a more mainstream version of English. Where non-standard grammar persists, it is my choice.

Amber helped more in my garden than everyone else put together. Discussions with her about farming, community, and food systems deeply influenced the course of my life. I attribute much of my growth and development in non-farming endeavors to Amber's influence. She handed me a guitar, saying that if I learned to play it, that I could keep it. I learned!

Landrace maxima squash

Landrace lettuce

Preface

I garden in a cold mountain valley in the desert. Warm-weather crops struggle. Crops like tomatoes, peppers, squash, and melons are difficult to grow. Varieties of vegetables and ways of doing things that work for an average gardener in an average climate don't work here. Methods and varieties that were popular many decades ago in far away gardens don't work for me.

To get a harvest on many warm weather crops, I had to develop varieties that are unique to my farm. Landrace varieties adapted most quickly to my growing conditions.

The first landrace crop that I grew did so well that I committed to applying the principles of landrace gardening to every plant and animal in my garden.

Crops grew as landraces since time immemorial, except during recent decades, when growing food was ceded to mega-corporations.

A landrace is a genetically-diverse, promiscuously-pollinating, and locally-adapted crop. Landraces are loved for producing stable yields under changing growing conditions.

Landrace crops arise by survival of the fittest and farmer preference for reliability in tough conditions. Plants that don't survive long enough to make seeds die out. The strongest plants survive. The arrival of new pests, new diseases, or changes in cultural practices, or in the environment may harm some individuals in a landrace population. With the high diversity many plant families do well, regardless of changing conditions.

Landrace crops frequently grow under subsistence level conditions without costly inputs such as herbicides, pesticides, fertilizers, or weeding. For gardens with extreme growing conditions or pests, landrace crops may provide the only reliable harvests.

The premise of this book is that growing food, saving seeds, and plant breeding are the common inheritance of humanity. Illiterate plant breeders brought us every crop that we now grow. The seedkeepers didn't read or write. They didn't know about genes. Without book-learning, they collaborated cooperatively with each other and with the plants and ecosystem to bring us wonderful crops.

The work these simple people did to develop corn, beans, squash, and grain is the most sophisticated and important thing humanity has accomplished. It hides in plain sight, dwarfing the achievement of the greatest temples in the world.

Landrace plant breeding is work best done by simple people. We don't need laboratories, or even literacy—the brilliance and magnitude of what we accomplish with just our hearts and minds, in community, is staggering.

The techniques of growing locally-adapted food and seed are as available to us today as they were in ancient times.

About 60 years ago, an industrial model of growing food began to separate people from traditional food production methods. Far-away "experts" replaced people's own understanding and insight. People generally stopped growing their own food and seeds, and became cogs in a global corporate machine. The separation is pervasive.

This book explains an alternate method, encouraging freedom and community self-sufficiency in food and seed production.

I prefer to garden with gentleness and loving awareness, towards myself, the plants, animals, and microbes. I don't treat us like cogs in an industrial machine. When I harvest seeds on a warm autumn day, my heart-song encompasses the people, plants, and ecosystem for thousands of years, into the past and future. My harvest techniques try to preserve the microbial symbiotes that the plants have nurtured.

The take-away message from this book is a message of hope. Food production, seed saving, and plant breeding are easily within reach of the average gardener and village. We do not need to depend on schooling, experts, far away mega-corporations, or their products.

We can grow excellent seeds that are locally adapted to thrive in our own gardens and communities.

Landrace gardening offers food security through biodiversity and promiscuous pollination.

Cache Valley, Utah

Joseph Lofthouse,
Paradise, Cache Valley, Rocky Mountains

xvii

1 Survival of the Fittest

Landrace gardening is the traditional method of growing food. It is based on survival of the fittest. Landrace varieties are locally adapted, genetically variable, and promiscuously-pollinating. This book focuses on the intimate connection of landrace varieties with local gardeners and communities.

Landraces adapt to changing conditions. The plants most likely to thrive are the offspring of plants that previously thrived.

When I plant seeds obtained from the industrialized seed system, it is common for 75% to 95% of the varieties to fail. My neighbors whine to me that my mongrel varieties thrive on once a week irrigation, while their catalog cultivars dry up and die, even with daily watering. When I ask where they got their seeds, they proudly tell me that they got them from an organic farm in coastal Oregon.

Our growing conditions are high-altitude brilliantly-sunlit super-arid desert, with huge day/night and seasonal temperature swings. The conditions where the seeds grew are overcast, low-elevation, damp, humid, with mild temperatures. The catalog seeds grew in a completely different region with many growing conditions the opposite of what we have here. The seeds lack the genetic skillset necessary to thrive in our conditions.

In a larger context, the vast majority of seed sold by the seed industry is unvetted seed. There is little, if any, disclosure or accountability about the seed's growing conditions. They could come from anywhere in the world, with different climates, soils, and ecosystems.

I get better results by growing bioregionally produced seeds. I get the best results from growing my own hyper-localized varieties. Not only are the seeds adapted to the climate and growing conditions, they are adapted to my habits as a farmer.

The first landrace crop that I grew was Astronomy Domine sweet corn. It was a breeding project by Alan Bishop of Bishop's Homegrown in Pekin, Indiana. The goal of the project was to create a hybrid swarm containing hundreds of varieties of sweet corn: modern hybrids, ancient landraces, and traditional heirlooms. When I planted the seeds, some died, and some thrived. Some got eaten by pheasants or skunks. Overall, the results were lovely. I saved seeds from the best, and replanted. The crop was fantastic. They were more robust, more colorful, more productive, and tastier than the commercial hybrid sweet corn my family had grown for decades.

Astronomy Domine sweet corn, first landrace harvest

A decade later, my version of Astronomy Domine is different from Alan's. Mine is shorter-season, with more colorful kernels. My strain matures ten days earlier than Alan's.

I fell in love with the sweet corn landrace, and converted my entire farm to landrace-style growing. Cantaloupe was a good crop to work with, because traditional melon varieties don't ripen before fall frosts. Highly outcrossing crops, like melons, adapt quickly to landrace growing. Outcrossing creates genetic diversity, providing opportunities to find new varieties that thrive on my farm.

To start the cantaloupe project, I saved seeds from the few melons that had produced a fruit the previous year. I added varieties: from local farm stands, the Internet, seed catalogs, grocery stores. Some varieties didn't germinate. Some varieties succumbed to bugs. Others didn't grow in the cold. Some grew robustly. The two best-growing plants produced more fruit than the rest of the patch combined.

It was obvious early in the growing season that some plants were thriving. Others grew slowly.

At the beginning of a landrace development project, I cull sparingly. I want anything that can make seed to contribute its genetics to the gene-pool. In later years, I select more for productivity and taste. Nuances regarding culling are covered in later chapters.

I collected seed and replanted. Oh, my heck!! I was used to trying to grow maladapted cantaloupes. I never imagined that cantaloupes could produce abundantly. I harvested a hundred pounds of fruit at a time!

I think of the third year of a landrace breeding project as the magical year. The first year, the totally maladapted plants die out. The second year, the survivors cross-pollinate. The third year their offspring are the best crossed with the best. Even without high crossing rates, the third year plants have two years of local adaptation and selection for greatness.

Susan Oliverson grows melons in the same mountain valley as I do. We shared seeds liberally with each other. I trust her seeds, because we share the same climate, soil, altitude, and bugs. We both value diversity. Her seeds thrive in my garden. We named the variety Lofthouse-Oliverson Landrace Muskmelon.

A key component of landrace gardening is community collaboration: locally, bioregionally, and from similar ecosystems around the world.

Spinach converted easily to landrace growing. I planted a number of varieties of spinach next to each other and culled the plants that were slow growing or quick to bolt. About 4 of the 12 varieties were suitable for my garden. I allowed them to cross-pollinate and set seed. A few years later, someone gave me a packet of spinach seeds. I

*Landrace vs. foreign spinach
(red box around foreign)*

planted it next to my locally-adapted landrace. The imported spinach went to seed at 3 inches (8 cm) tall. The landrace spinach had leaves a foot long.

Watermelon tasting

The watermelon project initially included collaborators from around the world. We shared seeds liberally among participants. The most reliable imports into my garden are from the nearest collaborators. Far-away collaborators, and large seed companies are important for gathering diversity. Genetically diverse, cross-pollinating crops rearrange their genetics to match local conditions.

To start the watermelon project, I planted around 700 seeds. The first planting included promiscuously pollinated hybrid offspring of hundreds of varieties. I harvested five fruits the first year. That is great odds for a survival of the fittest plant breeding program. One of those fruits was from the heirloom variety of watermelon that my daddy has preserved for decades in our valley.

Sometimes when I start adapting a new crop to my garden, I import hundreds of varieties, making a mass cross. Other times I take a slow and steady approach. I cover both methods in a later chapter.

Turnip-rooted parsnip

I took the slow and steady approach with parsnips. My soil becomes hard by fall. They were difficult to dig. They were breaking off. Most of the food value remained in the ground. We started with a turnip-rooted parsnip, allowing it to naturally cross-pollinate with a more vigorous, longer-rooted parsnip. Then we re-selected for the turnip-rooted shape. I'm unlikely to introduce long-rooted parsnips again. I don't want to lose the current shape.

In my experience planting these genetically-diverse crops, they cross-pollinate and undergo survival of the fittest selection. They breed themselves. My main function is to stay out of the way. I plant at an appropriate time, and irrigate or weed as needed. An entire chapter of this book is devoted to exploring promiscuous pollination.

I do not coddle plants. If a plant struggles with disease, or pests, I cull it. I do not try to save it with pesticides, sprays, herbicides, labor, or treatments. If I pull it early, then it doesn't shed pollen into the rest of the patch. I explore the nuances of this approach in the chapter on pests and diseases.

A lot of gardeners put huge amounts of labor and materials into growing tomatoes. They keep them off the soil. They trellis and prune them for airflow. They spray constantly. I grow tomatoes sprawling on the dirt. I ignore them. If a variety can't handle the local pests and diseases, or my hands-off methods, then I don't want it in my garden. I prefer to grow locally-adapted varieties that can handle the growing conditions exactly as they are today.

It is much easier for plants to modify their genetics than it is for me to change growing conditions. So I do not add fertilizer to my fields, nor try to modify the soil. If I fertilized, I would be selecting for plants that require fertilizer.

Transplanting is often detrimental to plants, so I grow by direct seeding if at all possible. Direct seeded crops grow much more robustly and reliably than transplants. The ability to survive and thrive when direct seeded is high on my list of selection priorities.

I dislike weeding. By not weeding, I select for plants that out-compete the weeds. When they get into a garden where people weed, they thrive. A number of years in a row, I lost my carrots to weeds. The carrots were slow to germinate. They grew slowly. The weeds overwhelmed them. I saved seed from the few plants that survived the weeds for several years in a row. The offspring became robust, quick-growing plants. I apply that sort of out-competing weeds strategy to every crop that I grow. I typically weed one time, shortly after germination.

Weeds provide significant food to me. It might be hard to tell, by watching me work in the garden, if I forage, or if I weed. Many of the weeds go directly from hand to mouth.

Survival of the fittest means surviving whatever the farmer or the environment throws at them.

Grown With Local Seeds

www.localseed.rocks

2 Freelance vs. Industry

Landrace gardening is about localized freelance food production, seed saving, and plant breeding. Throughout history, balance has shifted between small-scale food production and centralization. We are in an era where centralization has run its course. People are returning to decentralized food production. Locally-adapted seeds play a vital role in healthy food systems.

History and Politics

For 10,000 years, agriculture thrived by growing locally-adapted crops. Each gardener and farmer saved seeds from their own garden. Nearby gardeners shared seeds with each other. Food production and seed saving were local. Genetic diversity and cross-pollination allowed crops to adapt to changing conditions.

About 60 years ago, large corporations started breeding crops. They selected for uniformity and shipping qualities. They discarded most of the species' diversity using intense inbreeding. Pesticides, herbicides, fungicides, fertilizers, ripening agents, and preservatives compensated for the inbreeding and shipping needs.

The plants grown under that system lost much of their genetic memory of how to deal with pests, diseases, and adverse growing conditions. They became dependent on the synthetic chemicals.

Home gardeners are reluctant to poison their crops or themselves with chemicals. It is rare for a home gardener to stick to the strict spray schedules required to get the best yield out of highly inbred crops.

You get what you select for, even if the selection is unintentional. Gardeners that use compost, mulch, or wood-chips select for plants that grow best with those inputs. The industrialized seed industry selected for varieties that require inorganic fertilizer, crop protection chemicals, and weeding. When industrialized seeds grow outside those conditions, they struggle.

Genetically-diverse crops provide reliability despite changing conditions. Cross-pollinating varieties rearrange their genetics to make the best of new conditions.

Highly inbred or cloned crops contributed to massive crop failures including: The European potato pestilence of 1845-1857, the southern corn rust in Africa in the 1950s, the American corn blight of 1970, and the GMO corn failure in South Africa in 2009.

Coffee, bananas, wheat, apples, potatoes, and tomatoes are crops currently under threat of system wide disruption. I believe that the failure of new-fangled rice in India contributes to the high suicide rate among farmers.

Genetically diverse crops are less susceptible to whole-system collapses. I grow about 5000 types of sweet corn. A mega-farm might only grow one type. A single cob of my landrace sweet corn has more genetic diversity than hundreds of acres of commercial sweet corn.

Heirlooms are varieties that thrived on a far away farm many decades ago. Conditions are different today, and on my farm. I constantly generate varieties that could be called heirlooms 50 years from now.

A recent social disruption resulted in seed companies being unable to keep up with demand. They didn't have the staff, equipment, supplies, or seeds to supply everyone that wanted seeds. The grocery stores demonstrated the foibles of a globalized just-in-time delivery model, running out of many types of food and supplies. Some governments banned the sale of seeds as non-essential.

Growing locally-adapted crops as a community provides maximum food security and freedom. A community, that is growing its own food and seed, is less susceptible to actions by far away corporations or politicians.

Parable of the Hill People

People have known the basic facts about plant breeding for eons. Plants make seeds, which can be collected and replanted. Offspring resemble their parents and grandparents. With that foundation of knowledge, illiterate plant breeders domesticated the food species that we now grow.

Over tens of thousands of years, illiterate humans selected for plants and animals that were useful for food. They selected against poisons and excessive fibrousness. They selected for productivity, and for resistance to bugs and disease. They selected for great flavors and high nutritional content.

During that time, humans and plants entered into agreements with each other. The plants agreed to produce abundantly and to give up their poisons, thorns, and anti-nutrients. The humans agreed to care for, nurture, and protect the plants. Together, the plants and the humans entered into mutually beneficial symbiotic relationships.

In addition to the obviously observed symbiotic relationships, unseen symbiotic relationships also developed with the microbes that lived inside, and nearby, the people and the plants.

Some plants and some human cultures took the symbiosis to the next level. Humans became sedentary, and started staying near the grains to better protect them from predators and competition from weeds. The abundance of food allowed humans to spend more time on cultural pursuits, and less time on day to day survival.

The humans separated into civilized people who lived in cities near the grains, and hill people who lived more as nomads, or hunter-gatherers. The hill people also domesticated plants. They tended to practice perennial horticulture instead of annual agriculture.

The civilized people discovered that they could store grains for months, years, or decades. They gathered the grains into storehouses for safekeeping, and appointed strong men to guard the grain. Then, since the strong men had control of the grain, they demanded obeisance in exchange for food, sending out deputies to make sure that all the grain produced by the civilized folks ended up in the centralized granaries, and not in private pantries.

The hill people continued to live in their traditional ways, growing perishable foods that were not easily centralized or shipped. Growing small gardens that were not worth a bureaucrat's time. Foraging in the wildlands for foods that were not readily counted. Keeping mobile herds and flocks. Growing perennial crops that can go years between harvests, or annual crops that can fend for themselves.

The civilized folks industrialized their food production system, sending hoards of robots into the fields and warehouses, with just enough low-paid workers to keep the robots operational. They spewed poisons into the air, land, water, and themselves. The living soil turned into dead dirt, and the rivers and oceans into dead zones.

The industrialization of the food system decimated the microbes, fungi, and endophytes that the plants required for proper growth.

The crops grown by the civilized folks became imbeciles due to intense inbreeding. They lost the intelligence for dealing with environmental stress. Mechanization and overuse of crop protection chemicals, sprays, and fertilizers made the plants dependent on the robots, furthering the forgetfulness. The civilized plants grew poorly when planted in more natural gardens.

The civilized people also became dependent on the robots for their food. They came to obey anything that the strong men told them to do, so that they could continue to eat. The civilized people became hard, like the machines that fed them. Fear, mistrust, and despair filled their cities. They forgot how to sing and dance, preferring to watch other people sing and dance as shown to them by the robots.

The animals and crops grown by the hill people retained their genetic memory about how to deal with bugs, diseases, farmers, soils, and ecosystems. The people, and their plants, maintained healthy relationships with the weeds, animals, microbes, fungi, and endophytes. The intelligent, diverse crops grown by the hill people produced a rich abundance of healthy food, offering peace and freedom to the hill people.

The hill people frequently celebrated their good fortune, and the wisdom of their plant and human ancestors. They gathered together for singing, dancing and giving thanks for the beautiful flavors, robust plants, natural world, and their communities. Their music and dance was spontaneous, made with their own bodies, imaginations, and instruments. Joy, peace, and cooperation filled their villages.

Freelance permaculture:
Strawberry and mushroom

Seed Grown Plum

C4 Bitter, acidic, sour, citrus, bright

A4-2 Sour, astringent, lime, citrus, yuck!

A5-1 Mild, pleasant, melon, flat, fennel

Max-habro. Bright, wet dog, flavor
musk bomb, nutty, melon sour milk

C3 acidic, tang, Wow!
honeydew, sweet, melor

C5-5 Acidic, not funky, light, savory,
watery, most bland, fresh

C5-1 Sweet floral, bland,
fermenty, good balance

C5-Yellow Mild,bland, bleck,
low acid, mealy, low sugar

A1-1 Winner of taste testing.
Mango, XXX good, Wow! Best.

A4-3 No. Sour. Tart. Watery. Bland

A4-1 Juicy green, tart, great initial flavor, cucumber skin

C5-4 Melon, yum, funky & sweet, yum,

Tomato tasting party
Summary of comments from many taste testers

3 Continuous Improvement

The greatest benefit to me from growing landraces is that my crops thrive. They get better every year. Seeds that I grow myself grow more vigorously than what I can buy.

When I buy a variety from a multi-national seed company, I can't predict how it will grow in my garden. Seeds with different genetics can even carry the same label. If I plant three or four varieties and save the seeds from plants that grow best for me, I select for plants that thrive. They produce reliably year after year.

Multi-national companies test their seeds for average conditions in average gardens. That means that their seeds may not do as well as seeds that are tailored for specific conditions in specific gardens.

I believe that if we want the best cultivars for our own gardens, we should grow genetically-diverse, promiscuously-pollinating crops, then save seeds from them in our own gardens and communities. My farm has extreme growing conditions due to the high altitude and short season. I could not reliably grow many warm weather crops until I started saving my own seeds.

A friend was growing zucchini squash in my garden. She planted commercial seeds that were not locally adapted. They were a magnet for disease and bugs. They died quickly. My squash seem impervious to pests and diseases. Therefore, it was joyful for me to watch the demise of her squash. They say that it's inappropriate to gloat in another's misfortune. In this case, I made an exception, because it was lovely to get such a simple demonstration of the benefits of landrace gardening.

Reliability and Productivity

I love the reliability and productivity of landrace crops. The ancestors for a number of generations grew and produced seeds on my farm. Because offspring resemble their parents and grandparents, the seeds produced on my farm usually thrive. The ancestors have already demonstrated that they have what it takes to survive.

As the climate changes from year to year, a genetically-diverse, promiscuously-pollinating variety adjusts to the changing conditions.

I can't trust seeds grown in far away countries or farms. They were grown in a different ecosystem.

I can trust seeds grown in my own garden, or in my neighbor's gardens. They have demonstrated that they are well suited for my mountain valley.

First year (immature) winter squash

Most commercial varieties fail in my garden. In the first generation, a few plants may produce seeds before the fall frosts. The basic requirement for landrace growing is planting locally grown seeds. Seeds from immature fruits are often viable enough for some to germinate.

In later years, the crop moves towards earlier harvest. The third season is when the genetics have undergone the initial selection, and crossing, and the plants begin to thrive.

In the first three years of the moschata squash landrace, early frosts killed the plants 88 and 84 days after planting. That provided strong selection towards shorter days to maturity.

The selection for quicker maturity in Astronomy Domine sweet corn happened gradually over five years. Selection happened both by my choice, and inadvertently.

I select for shortened days to maturity, because the short season is a primary reason why commercial seeds don't grow well for me.

Selection for quicker maturity happens both by natural selection, and by farmer and community choice. Quicker maturing crops are more reliable. People in hot-weather areas tell me that the quick maturing trait works for them too. They can season shift and grow two crops in a year. They can harvest a crop quickly before it is destroyed by bugs, disease, weather, or

Third year (mature) winter squash

animals. Later on in the book, there is a section devoted to season shifting.

Selection happens quickest in genetically diverse varieties that are cross-pollinating. Genetic diversity is important, because it gives the plants genetic tools to try different ways of coping with the world. Promiscuity (where seeds are from pollination between two plants not closely related) is important because the plants can try new genetic combinations more quickly.

There is a table in the appendix that recommends varieties based on ease of converting to landrace style growing. I write about how to facilitate crossing among the rarely crossing species in the chapter on promiscuous pollination.

Developing landrace varieties is quickest with outcrossing species like corn, squash, melons, cucumber, spinach, favas, runner beans, and brassicas. Outcrossing is defined as readily sharing pollen with each other.

Better Tasting Food

By saving my own seeds, year after year, based on what tastes best to me, I develop pleasant tasting strains of vegetables.

Industrialized varieties often taste horrible to me. I wonder how people can tolerate such bland-tasting pseudo-food? Many of the species of fresh fruits and vegetables offered by the grocery stores are unpalatable to me.

When the university conducted a survey of my customers, I was startled about their primary reason for buying my food. I thought they would say because it was organically grown, or because it was locally produced. Perhaps because it was picked the evening before market. Nope! People were primarily buying my vegetables because of the flavor. I started paying close attention to breeding for delightful flavors.

To maintain and improve the taste of my crops, I taste every fruit before saving seeds from it. I don't save seeds from dull-tasting parents. After a few years, the tastes became tailored to my body, and my likes and dislikes. I believe that my food preferences represent typical primate behavior. By selecting for flavors that appeal to me, I select for flavors that please my community.

I ask the local people that eat my food, "If anything tastes extraordinary, please return seeds to me." Chefs return seeds from fruits that taste great, along with a piece of the fruit. I also taste it. They cull seeds from fruits that they don't like. I ask the same

High carotenes taste great

from friends, family, and community. In that way, the flavors become a community selection project, and not just one farmer's idiosyncrasies.

There are many factors that contribute to the culinary profile of a vegetable: fibrousness, mouth feel, sweetness, bitterness, color, aroma, texture, and more. I pay attention to all them.

I love the taste of highly colored carotenes in my food. When I select for squash that are bright orange, they are tastier.

Beta-readers of this book suggested that I describe the taste of carotenes. I can't pinpoint a particular flavor. When I eat high carotene foods, I feel contentment, joy, and satisfaction. It feels like my body is releasing a flood of feel-good chemicals, to encourage me to seek out similar foods.

Over the years, I inadvertently selected for squash that are easy to cut. Because I taste every fruit before saving seeds from it, I'm also cutting every fruit. If a squash was too hard to cut, or to chew, I'd toss it into the compost rather than save seeds from it. Therefore, the squash became a joy to use in the kitchen.

Just like the squash, the muskmelons became much more colorful and tasty over the years. When I first started growing melons, I called them cantaloupes, because that was what the seed packet called them. That is what they call the things in the grocery store that have a similar appearance. These days, I call them muskmelons, because they are not the same thing as the stores are selling. My melons are hyper-aromatic. They are sweet as can be. The texture is melt-in-the-mouth soft. The flavors are robust. I might lose 20% of the fruits before I can get them to market. The joyful flavors and aroma more than make up for the losses.

I really dislike bitter lettuce, and therefore it is my intent to taste every lettuce plant before saving seeds from it. If a plant tastes bitter, I cull it. The bitterness in lettuce is a poison. The first time I did this tasting, on several hundred lettuce plants, I made myself sick. I got more careful about tasting the lettuce. Only the tiniest taste, and spitting immediately after. Eventually, I learned that thick milky sap is a sign that the lettuce is bitter. Tasting is less important these days. I can do the inspection visually.

Less Stress

By growing my own landrace seeds I eliminate stresses. I don't have to worry about paying for seeds, poisons, or fertilizers. Records or pedigrees are optional. I don't have to keep seeds pure, or isolated. I can save seeds from hybrids, and let varieties get mixed up. I don't get out of kilter when the seed catalog drops my favorite variety, or if a variety name or most recent story gets lost. I don't worry about getting a harvest. I don't worry about supply chain interruptions.

Modern inbred varieties rely on synthetic chemicals for crop protection. Landraces rely on genetic variability for crop security.

I devote a section to plant purity, isolation distances, and minimum population sizes later in the book. I won't dwell much on them here, other than to say that the recommendations commonly given in gardening books are intended for mega seed companies growing to supply the entire world. Standards are different for someone who's growing seed for their own garden or village.

If Queen Anne's lace contaminates my carrot seed crop, I weed out the few percent of undesirable seedlings. No harm done. No worries. No stress.

I choose to minimize record keeping. I limit records to a description of the variety on the seed storage jar, and the year grown. When I grow sister lines, which are hard to tell apart in the field, it would help if I made a planting map, so that I know which line I grew. I take lots of pictures of the garden while it's growing. Other than that, I choose to minimize stress by not keeping records. All the varieties that I currently grow were developed by seedkeepers that weren't keeping written records. I prefer doing plant breeding as an artist, instead of as a scientist. I sing for the plants. I dance in the fields. I take artsy photos. I host festivals and parties to honor the seasons, the plants, the soil, and the water. I make musical instruments from the plants.

When I grow crops landrace style, it is fine to save seeds from some types of hybrids. The offspring may be variable, they may have genetic problems like male sterility. I don't have to stress about those things. There is plenty of time later on to select for traits that I adore.

I don't stress about keeping varieties pure, or contaminating them. With landrace gardening, getting things mixed up is a virtue.

The first thing I do when getting a new variety, is to forget the current name and most recent story. That eliminates the stress of keeping track of the names and stories. It is joyful to let each plant tell its current story in each generation. The story of each variety stretches back tens of thousands of years, through thousands of seedkeepers. It slights them to only tell the tiny fraction of the story associated with a variety name on a seed packet.

I have crop failures as a landrace gardener. They are less frequent than when I was buying random seeds.

Some crop families thrive during hotter, drier summers. Other families do better in cooler, damper summers. By growing crops from several families, I hedge my risk of every family failing in the same growing season.

I worry less about supply chain interruptions due to disasters or politics. There is still risk, because many of my crops depend on irrigation. I grow some species by alternate methods that don't require irrigation. This book contains a chapter later on that explores alternative growing methods and crops.

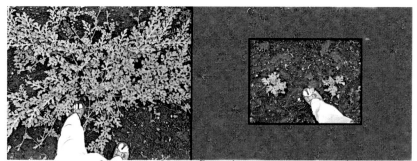

Watermelon: Landrace (huge) vs. commercial (tiny)
Planted the same day, a few feet apart

Awesome-tasting daylily flowers

Zucchini: Summer or winter squash

4 Heirlooms, Hybrids, and Landraces

This chapter explores the different terms used to describe how seeds grow, and what the phrases mean. The seed keeping world often uses words in ways that are contrary to their plain meaning. People assign values of good or evil to the terms, and then refuse to use seed that is perfectly wonderful, because they believe it might be evil. Or they seek out saintly seeds, not realizing that saints arise as a response to darkness.

Heirlooms

An heirloom is a variety that has been highly inbred for decades, and is maintained by continual inbreeding. It may have been the perfect variety for one family or tribe, that lived a very long time ago, in a place far, far away. Because heirlooms are from a far different place and time, they often lack the genetic toolkit to deal with modern conditions. They may have an alluring story, which may or may not be factually true. The stories don't contribute to a plant's growth, productivity, or flavor. A story about an inbred variety from long ago and far away doesn't feed the community. The stories that feed a community, are about our loving, heart-felt participation in the ongoing web of life, in all its ever-changing configurations.

I dislike heirloom preservation. It leads to "inbreeding depression," which is the loss of vigor an organism experiences from being inbred.

I think that the best possible method of heirloom preservation is to be actively growing crops and saving seeds. Allowing the genetics to flow and shift with the climate, the pests, the farmer's habits, and community preferences is how seeds have been preserved since seed-keeping began.

Open Pollinated

The claim regarding "open pollinated" varieties is that you can save the seeds from them, and they will look the same next year as they did last year. Open pollinated varieties persist through inbreeding. The emotional and common sense meaning of the phrase, is that there might be some crossing going on, leading to genetic diversity. However, in practice, the plants are isolated to prevent crossing from occurring. Varieties that are consistently isolated lose genetic diversity. The low genetic diversity is why they look the same from year to year. If they were crossing, they wouldn't stay the same.

I use the terms promiscuously-pollinated, inter-pollinated, and cross-pollinated. I want to emphasize that genetic diversity is encouraged. I don't use the term "open-pollinated" because I want to clearly distinguish between the inbreeding meme of "open-pollinated" and the outcrossing system preferred by landrace gardening.

The rate of cross-pollination varies widely between species, and even within varieties of the same species. I inter-plant different varieties to encourage outcrossing to whatever degree a variety is able to cross.

Replanting seeds from naturally occurring crosses selects for higher cross-pollination rates. In like manner, preserving heirloom purity selects for lower cross-pollination rates.

F1 Hybrids

Hybrids occur whenever two plants cross with each other that are not closely related. The seed industry is fond of taking two highly inbred parents and crossing them together. This results in offspring with highly uniform traits, which are approximately a blending of the traits of the parents, and sometimes with a particular trait of one parent being dominant.

In the next generation, the genes rearrange, and the traits of the grandparents get randomly distributed between the offspring. If the starting varieties were diverse, then this generation is likewise diverse as the blending traits and the dominant traits recombine in new ways.

The hybrids made by the mega-seed companies descend from highly inbred lines; therefore, the appearance of diversity is more of a token than a reality. Nevertheless, I love growing the offspring of commercial hybrids, because new phenotypes and genetic combinations are common.

Plants lose vigor due to inbreeding. Sometimes people talk about hybrid vigor. They gush over it like it is a good thing. What it really means, is that the hybrid grows better than either of its highly inbred parents. It doesn't mean that the hybrid grows better than plants that were never inbred. A more accurate description of this phenomenon is "partially reversing inbreeding depression."

Some hybrids made by commercial hybridizers are male sterile. They don't produce pollen because of a defect in the organelles of the plant. The organelles transfer only from the mother; therefore, the sterility is permanent. The phenomenon is called cytoplasmic male sterility. It is used because it is an inexpensive way to make hybrids, because the male sterile flowers produce eggs but no pollen, and cannot self-pollinate. The price to be paid for the cheapness is that the offspring are permanently male sterile.

In some cases, there are genes that can restore fertility. Paying attention to things like restorer genes is messy. I prefer to have fully functional plants in my garden, therefore, I routinely examine the flowers in my garden, and cull plants that don't have anthers, or that have defective anthers. On carrot flowers, the anthers are commonly missing in male sterile plants.

Male-sterile carrot　　　　　*Fertile carrot*

Before I was aware of cytoplasmic male sterility, 70% of my carrot landrace was male sterile. They grew fine. The fertile plants produced more than enough pollen. It seems undesirable to grow partially sterile plants. Each year I examine my carrot landrace and chop out plants that are missing anthers. I take care when importing new varieties into my garden.

Commercial hybrids of the following species generally contain cytoplasmic male sterility: Broccoli, cabbage, radish, onion, carrot, beet and sunflower. I recommend that commercial hybrids of these species not be included in a landrace garden. Additional varieties are listed in the appendix.

Hybrids of brassicas may also be made using self incompatibility. I may use them after examining the flowers for normal pollen production.

Hybrids of the following crops are generally free of cytoplasmic male sterility: tomato, cucumber, squash, corn, watermelon, melons and spinach.

Another trait that commercial hybrids carry, is that they have become dependent on synthetic chemicals and fertilizers. They may fail to thrive when grown in organic systems. I only add water to my garden. I don't want my plants dependent on costly inputs.

The parents of commercial hybrids have been selected to produce great offspring. The grandchildren are likely to be great plants. A lot of work went into identifying those traits. We might as well incorporate them into our landrace gardens, as long as they don't carry deleterious traits.

Freelance Hybrids

I use the term "freelance hybrids" to describe the ad hoc hybrids that are made by gardeners using human labor. They may be made artistically without following rigorous protocols.

For the small scale farmer and gardener, making home-grown hybrids is readily accomplished with simple tools and techniques. Move pollen from one plant, and apply it to the stigma of another. The plant parts can be small. With the right magnifying and manipulation tools, the process is straight-forward.

Freelance hybrids can be made to combine traits from different varieties into one new variety. They can be made for playfulness and exploration. They could even be made for productivity or profit. I give some examples later in this chapter.

When we make manual freelance hybrids, we increase diversity and local adaptation.

We can make freelance hybrids within and between species. This chapter ends by describing some of my personal favorites.

Plant biology is fuzzy. Industrialized humans like things to be black and white. The biological world is nuanced. There are many shades of gray surrounding every aspect of biology. This is especially apparent when we play with making hybrids from genetically diverse parents.

Promiscuous Hybrids

In the crops that I grow, I encourage promiscuous pollination. This means interplanting varieties with different physical characteristics, or phenotypes, so that they can more easily cross. I don't have a DNA laboratory. I don't know what genetics my crops have. If I plant seeds from different phenotypes, I figure that I'm getting genetic diversity. In the highly outcrossing crops like corn, cucurbits, and spinach, it's their nature to be promiscuous.

Tomatoes, peas, flax, lettuce, grains, and common beans are mostly in-breeding and don't produce many hybrids. Cross-pollination rates are around 0.5% to 10% depending on weather, insect populations, and variety. Selection for purity and inbreeding inadvertently contributed to these low crossing rates. The appendix contains a list of cross-pollination rates for common species.

Whenever a rare natural hybrid appears among them, I give them a special place in the garden. Planting the offspring of hybrids allows more opportunities to find plants that really thrive in my garden. If I plant seeds from the naturally occurring hybrids, I'm selecting for plants that have a higher chance of crossing than their peers.

Lettuce: Wild (left), hybrid (middle), domestic (right)

Most wheat plants don't expose anthers to the wind, but I notice some wheat plants with many anthers outside the flower. I could rapidly select for higher outcrossing if I marked the plants with exposed anthers, and preferentially replanted those seeds.

To encourage outcrossing, I also watch tomato flowers, and replant those with the most open flower types.

The offspring of the naturally hybridized plants get their genetics rearranged, which provides more opportunities for the plant to learn how to better deal with the ecosystem, the farmer, and the community.

My great-great grandfather, James Lofthouse, discovered a naturally-occurring hybrid in his wheat field. He saved seed from it, growing it in his kitchen garden to increase seed. He released it publicly in about 1890. Eventually it became the most widely planted wheat in northern Utah and southern Idaho. I still grow "Lofthouse Wheat." My family still benefits from the good will that was generated because James replanted seeds from a hybrid

James Lofthouse

and attached our family name to the resulting landrace.

Because of the highly localized nature of pollination, I encourage the creation of natural hybrids, by planting different varieties close to each other. When I plant dry bush beans, I plant them jumbled up. The crossing rate might be as low as 1 in 200. I find new crosses each year because of the close spacing, and because I'm looking for them.

Heritage Landraces

A genetically-diverse, promiscuously-pollinating landrace combines the best of all worlds, creating new hybrids between locally adapted parents, while maintaining local adaptation and the emotional satisfaction of growing inter-pollinating crops.

When people ask if my crops are heirlooms, I say no, because that implies that they have been inbreeding for 50 years. I call my crops "heritage varieties." It implies that the crops grow in the same way that people have always grown crops.

Like generations of farmers before me, I till my fields once in the fall, and once immediately before planting in the spring. I currently farm three-quarters of an acre. I do not own land. I grow on vacant lots, using whatever fields are available in my community. At one time, I was farming four acres scattered across eight fields in several communities, which gave me lots of isolation options. I sprinkle irrigate for 12 weeks during the hottest part of the summer. I am not selecting for drought tolerance, only for tolerance to dry desert air and brilliant sunlight.

Soil fertility is maintained by growing lots of weeds, which are returned to the soil where they grew. I plant in widely separated rows, to give plenty of room to seed-producing crops. For most species, I plant rows between 10 to 50 feet long. I plant about 150 to 500 row feet of corn, beans, and squash. The larger plantings are because they are staple crops for my community.

Examples

Some hybrids are easier to make than others, because of the nature of the plants. Corn and squash produce hundreds of seeds per manual pollination. The male and female flowers are separate, making it easy to move pollen manually.

Garbanzo beans produce one or two seeds per attempted pollination. The male and female parts are in the same small flower, and close together, making it hard to produce hybrids with garbanzo beans.

Corn

Corn hybrids are super easy to make. They can be made by planting different varieties side by side, and then pulling the tassels off the female parent before they release pollen. Tassels are sneaky. I like to de-tassel by walking up the row on both sides and from both directions, and repeat frequently. I plant two to four rows of mother plants for each row of pollen donors.

I like combining the great taste and reliability of old-fashioned sweet corn with the sugary enhanced trait. I call it Paradise, after my village. Sugary enhanced sweet corn is difficult for me to grow, because the seeds rot in cool spring soil. The old-fashioned sweet corn germinates reliably and grows vigorously. I use the old-fashioned sweet corn Astronomy Domine as the mother, and a sugary enhanced sweet corn such as Who Gets Kissed or Ambrosia as the pollen donor father. The Paradise offspring inherit the strong seed-coat of the mother, and additional sweetness from the father. The days to maturity of the hybrid may shift by choosing a pollen donor with longer or shorter days to maturity. Offspring mature mid-way between the parent's maturity dates.

When I make hybrids available, I freely publish the identities of the parents. If people like the seed, they can either recreate it for themselves in large quantities, or buy small quantities from me. It's common for a corn plant to produce around 600 seeds. It is easy to produce enough seed to plant a field of hybrid corn.

Spinach

Freelance spinach hybrids are easy. The species produces male plants and female plants, and is wind-pollinated. To make a hybrid, plant two varieties side by side. Cull the male plants from one variety before they flower. The seeds

Female Male

Flowering spinach

on the mother plants from that variety are inter-variety hybrids. The other variety remains pure.

Distinguish male spinach plants by their smaller size. The male flowers look fuzzy, and wave around in the wind at the top of the plant. Female plants are larger. The nondescript female flowers occur lower on the plant, and close to the stem.

Squash

Squash hybrids are easy to make, because the huge flowers are easy to work with, and flowers are either male or female.

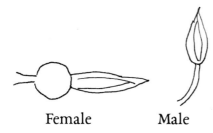

Female   Male

Squash flowers

Seal the flowers with clips or tape the evening before they open. Female flowers already have a small fruit attached. Keeping the flowers closed prevents insects from spreading pollen. In the morning, use the male flower to apply pollen to the female flower. Close the flower to keep bugs out. Mark the fruit by tying a ribbon to the peduncle.

Hybrid squash with parents

I really like the freelance hybrid between Hubbard and Banana. As a plant breeding project, the second generation combines the traits of the grandparents in every possible combination. Beginning with dissimilar parents is a wonderful strategy for starting to explore plant breeding. Select for what you love.

Another way to make squash hybrids is to consistently remove the male flowers, so that all the pollen comes from other plants.

The path to victory is
not quarreling with evil...

It is doing what we love!

5 Creating Landraces

Modern landraces arise either by making an initial mass cross between many varieties, or by a slow and gradual process of adding new genetics from time to time.

To begin a breeding effort, I recommend using primarily heirlooms and open pollinated varieties. Some hybrids are acceptable.

Importing a landrace from elsewhere is a great way to trial a lot of diversity with little expense. In a 100-seed packet of my dry bush beans, there might be 40 distinct types. Some family is likely to thrive wherever it gets planted.

The starting seeds may not be locally or regionally adapted. They can still be a valuable source of genetic diversity. Some seed companies offer mixed varieties, for example 5 varieties of radish in the same seed packet. This is an inexpensive way to add diversity to a landrace. A 15-bean soup mix from the grocery store is an amazing value when used as seed stock.

Seeds grown by neighbors and local farmers are a treasure. They are already at least a year ahead in adapting to our conditions. I love seeds acquired from a local farmer's market where the farmers can only sell vegetables grown on their farm.

Due to cytoplasmic male sterility, I recommend that hybrids not be used in the creation of landraces for carrot, cabbage, broccoli, onion, beet, and potato. The following species are useful as hybrids: spinach, melon, squash, and tomato. I recommend routine screening to cull plants that don't have anthers.

The appendix contains a table that ranks species based on how easily they convert to landrace gardening, and notes if male sterility is common in particular species.

Grex

A grex is a bunch of varieties growing together. To create a grex, plant approximately equal amounts of seed from different sources and varieties. It is common to plant together the seeds from 5-50 varieties to make an original mass cross, which is called a grex.

Over time, a grex becomes a new proto-landrace. The landrace habituates to each garden and to each region by survival of the fittest, and farmer-directed selection. Landraces that have been selected to thrive in my arid, sunny, high-altitude garden grow much better than off-the-shelf seeds produced in far away climates with different soils, bugs, diseases, and farming practices.

It's common in my garden for about 75% to 95% of new foreign varieties to fail at producing seed.

Incremental Change

Landrace crops may arise gradually, by saving seeds from whatever survives this year and planting the collected seeds, then by planting a new variety in the next row over. If the new variety grows well, add its seeds to the landrace.

Landraces may start from accidental cross-pollination. Before I knew about landraces, an off-type squash appeared in my Burgess Buttercup. The fruits had always been dark green. An orange fruit showed up. Perhaps it was a naturally occurring hybrid with Red Kuri. I don't like the flavor, nor the low productivity of Red Kuri. The new hybrid looked wonderful. It tasted wonderful. It was productive. What's not to love about that? Therefore, I replanted the seeds from the new hybrid buttercup, and stopped planting Burgess. I called it Lofthouse Buttercup (version 2 of my buttercup).

Version 2 (left side)
Version 3 (right side)

A few years later, Hopi White crossed into the buttercup from several hundred feet away. It contributed genes for light skin tone. I re-selected for the fabulous buttercup flavor, and buttercup shape. I preferentially replanted seeds for the new colors. I didn't give it a new name, I continue to call it Lofthouse Buttercup (version 3).

My popcorn originated as a natural cross between a plain yellow popcorn, and a decorative multi-colored flour corn. I love multicolored kernels in popcorn. This is a cross that I wouldn't make intentionally, because it took a lot of effort to re-select for great popping.

It's easier if I don't introduce traits that have to be culled later. I'm careful to not grow hot peppers next to the sweet peppers. Some hot peppers grow well at my place. It could be really advantageous to cross them with sweet peppers, and then re-select for sweet, non-hot peppers. I don't want to create extra work.

Yellow crookneck squash

Stability

I like multi-colored, and multi-shaped fruits. I also like the comfort of old friends. When I created a crookneck squash landrace, I included about a dozen varieties of crookneck. One of them was from the amazingly diverse Long Island Seed Project. Ken Ottinger was making genetically-diverse inter-pollinating crops long before I encountered the idea.

I want my yellow crookneck to be perfectly yellow, and perfectly crooked-necked, like those from my childhood. I don't care what the leaves look like, or if the plants are semi-vining instead of bush. I select for the traits that I value, and let everything else be variable.

My muskmelons are selected for netted skin, and orange flesh. They are the same species as honeydew melons, which have smooth skin and green flesh. I want the nostalgia of traditional looking muskmelons. I grow green-fleshed melons in a different field, to keep them from crossing.

Stable muskmelons

Purple Top White Globe turnip

I maintain turnips as "Purple Top, White Globe." I haven't been interested in adding other colors of turnips.

My landraces can have as much stability, or as much variability as I like. I usually choose diverse phenotypes. Sometimes I value stability.

With corn, I crossed hundreds of varieties of corn together: Races from South America, heirlooms from North America, popcorn, sweet corn, flint corn, flour corn. Then I re-selected for each of those types. These days if I add a flour corn to my patch, I add it only to the flour corn. I'm keeping stability centered around the soft-kerneled flour corn phenotype.

Record Keeping

A strategy that works really well for me is to do landrace seed saving as an artist, rather than as a scientist. I worked as an analytical chemist for decades. I kept detailed, meticulous records. I began breeding plants with a scientist mindset.

Each crop generated hundreds of seed packets per year, and many pages of notes and photographs. It was overwhelming and discouraging. When I realized that I was spending more time keeping records than growing, I stopped the record keeping immediately. These days, all the seeds from a crop go into the same jar. Hundreds of seed packets became one bottle of seeds per crop. That freed up time to sing, dance, and play in the garden. I enjoy doing plant breeding as an artist.

At a seed conference, a friend had 1000 varieties of beans on the table. Each variety was carefully segregated into a separate container. She teased me, saying, "Joseph also brought 1000 varieties of beans." I held up a mason jar filled with 1000 varieties of beans, jumbled together. I plant, grow, harvest, and cook them together. Some stay firm when cooked. Others soften to make a rich broth. A delightful combination of traits.

Beans typically self-pollinate. Any type could be separated from the rest and easily converted into a cultivar.

The crops that I grow were domesticated primarily by people who could neither read nor write. When I don't keep records, I join a tradition older than agriculture.

I rejoice in letting go of attachments to names and stories. It frees me up to have a personal, intimate connection to the seeds. It helps me to more honestly evaluate each plant on its own merits, because I'm not biased by names or stories. Each relationship is fresh and new in each generation.

Seed Swaps

Seed swaps represent an inexpensive way to add genetic diversity to landrace crops. I don't care much about specific traits of specific cultivars. I seek genetic diversity. Then the plants and ecosystem do survival of the fittest selection. I don't like to mix sweet corn with flour corn. Within broad guidelines like that, pretty much any kind of seed is welcome to try to add its genes to my landraces.

Seed swap

I might only plant 10 seeds of each new variety. I might plant 5 to 100 varieties. I end up with lots of packets of leftover seed. I often gift the opened packets in seed swaps, or exchange them for something else.

People send me gifts of unwanted seeds. They send me 1000 seeds when I only want to plant a dozen. I receive many more seeds than I can grow. They aren't locally adapted. They are unlikely to survive my growing conditions. I don't like to throw them out, because life is precious. Often times, I gift those seeds at swaps.

Another way I deal with the excess seeds from swaps is to open the seed packets, and dump them into a jar. Sometimes by species, and sometimes many species lumped together. Then I plant a pinch of that seed in a field to see if anything amazing shows up. I may scatter it in the non-cultivated areas of the farm. Once in a while a species gets established, or reproduces. It may get added to one of my landraces.

People send me a lot of home-grown seed. Sometimes they are listed as "might be cross-pollinated." I love those kinds of exchanges! The more kinds of parents that are in a seed packet, the more opportunities there are to find a family group that thrives.

Jennifer's runner beans

If I get seed labeled "landrace" then happy, happy, joy, joy. While it might not be locally-adapted to my garden, there may be tremendous genetic diversity. Some family might be happy with the local ecosystem, and provide useful genetics. I planted runner beans many years in a row without success, until Holly Dumont sent me a packet of landrace runner beans. About 20% of them survived and made seed. That was enough to start a landrace runner bean breeding project.

A beta reader of this book was Jennifer Willis. She lives in my village. She has been growing landrace runner beans for 15 years. We swapped runner beans after she found out I want them. She got them from the UPS man.

Runner beans are precious to me, because they were the first seed crop I harvested, with my grandpa, when I was about four years old.

Neighborhood Exchange

Landrace varieties are deeply intertwined with the community in which they grow. I enjoy trading with the local neighbors. I might swap one kind of dry bean for another. My daddy has grown Charleston Gray watermelon for decades. It thrives in his garden. I ask for seeds from him often.

Each winter, I visit my regular trading partners. We compare notes and swap seeds. I take local seeds to the farmer's market. People bring seeds from their gardens to trade for something I'm growing. I really like this kind of trade. The locally-adapted varieties that my neighbors grow perform better than seeds from far away growers.

I do seed exchanges regularly with people who are working on landrace crops and who live in ecosystems similar to mine. I'll plant anything they send me. We have a history of collaboration.

Seed exchange

This sort of mutual-aid seed sharing is at the core of landrace gardening. An individual can maintain a landrace. It's much better when it's maintained by a community.

Seed Libraries

Custodians of seed libraries sometimes express angst. "What if the seeds that people bring back have been contaminated? What if they aren't pure?"

To me, that would be something that should be a treasured trait of the library, not something to be fearful about. Locally adapted seeds are a great thing to have in a library!

My strategy about genetically diverse landrace crops is to offer full disclosure to people about what they are getting. I do not offer uniform, distinct, nor stable seed, and I state that clearly and often. I offer biodiversity, and local adaptation.

6 New Methods and Crops

The magic of landrace plant breeding is that we are able to select for genetics that work with our habits and way of doing things. We don't have to grow crops in the same way they have always been grown. We could eat different parts of the plant. We could grow them at different times of year. We can select plants that fit the farmer's habits and preferred way of doing things.

The photo on the opposite page is from my red-podded pea project. I knew that red-podded peas were theoretically possible. There were no red-podded pea seeds for sale. Therefore, I created them by manually crossing yellow-podded peas with purple-podded peas. A small percentage of the offspring were red-podded. If I were to recreate this project, I would select the parents more carefully, to minimize extraneous traits. For example, I would choose parents that are both snow peas.

Inadvertent Selection

Growing plants and saving seeds is inadvertently or deliberately selecting for a population that thrives under the growing conditions they experienced. We can mold the population deliberately to give us what we want. We can wing it and get only inadvertent selection. The inbreeding nature of many domesticated crops is partially due to farmer's inadvertent selection against cross-pollination.

A plant's genetics gives it intelligence about coping with its environment. By growing them using our preferred methods, we are selecting for plants that grow best using those methods.

I reviewed seed production operations that used plastic extensively, both under and over the plants. The farmers were unaware that their methods select for plants that grow best when grown with plastic. Thus, when the plants get to customer's gardens who don't use plastics, the plants may fail. The plants lack a critical component of their accustomed environment. If the seed growers were intentional about the use of plastic, and advertised the plants as requiring plastic, that could be a blessing to their customers who use plastic. I feel it's a disservice to their customers to not disclose the risks.

A friend at farmer's market asked why her tomatoes get dirty, and mine stay clean. I didn't have an answer for her. Next time I picked tomatoes, I noticed that the landrace tomatoes have a

Self-cleaning tomatoes

different type of vine than commercially available tomatoes. When I'm saving seed from tomatoes, I don't save seeds from fruits that are laying in the mud. I had inadvertently selected for tomatoes that have an arching vine structure that keeps the fruits off the ground. The tomatoes took care of it themselves without any labor or attention from me.

Recently, I found a family of tomatoes that grow like shrubbery, with woody stems. I intend to explore that trait. I grow tomatoes sprawling on the ground, without trellising, or sprays. For people in damp climates, it would be clever to grow tomato shrubs that keep their leaves above blight infested soil.

I observe growers of tomatoes applying all manner of fertilizers, sprays, techniques, trellises, and labor. By doing so, they are inadvertently selecting for varieties that require those kinds of costly inputs.

Season Shifting

We can select crops that grow at a different season of the year than usual. I focus on selecting for crops that thrive when fall planted. I want an early harvest first thing in the spring. Crops like that could grow without irrigation in my ecosystem. Most of our moisture falls during frosty weather in fall, winter, and early spring.

Cold-tolerant crops that might overwinter and produce early spring food include: pea, lettuce, turnip, bok choi, kale, spinach, grains, chard, brassicas, and wild species. I plant annuals in the fall just before the fall monsoons. The weather screens for winter-hardiness. Some species and some specific varieties are more winter hardy than others. By selecting for winter hardiness, I may be selecting for traits that are detrimental in summer grown plants. Therefore, I split landraces into fall-planted or spring-planted sister lines.

Fall-planted grains can be grown without irrigation in my ecosystem. Rye is very winter hardy. Many varieties of wheat are winter hardy. Oats and barley have not been reliably winter hardy for me. By selecting for grains that thrive when fall planted, I make my farming less dependent on irrigation. I'm less beholden to the political and industrial machines that make pressurized irrigation possible. Alas, the acequias that moved open-ditch irrigation water throughout the community here are long gone.

In my ecosystem, rye is a self-seeding feral species. It does not require planting, weeding, or irrigation. Just harvest the mature grain. Some strains of wheat or barley might be suitable for similar treatment. Rye is tall. It outgrows the weeds. The grains are allelopathic. They poison other plants. They grow all winter, and thus out-compete the spring-germinating annuals.

Wheat has a lot of diversity in height. If intending to grow feral wheat, I would plant the tallest available varieties. They outgrow the weeds better, and minimize stooping during harvest.

There are a lot of biennial and perennial species that produce food in early spring. I have selected for parsnip, turnip, chard, carrot, and sunroot that overwinter without protection. Beet might adapt to fall planting.

Chickweed produces early spring greens. I would love to move it from a self-seeding annual into a deliberately planted crop. It already thrives here. It grows like a weed! With observation, and modest effort, it could become an important and reliable food crop, because it grows in super cold weather.

In warmer climates, the season can be shifted by planting at a time of year when a specie's primary predators and diseases are not active. Rather than growing a full season squash, a short season squash might grow earlier or later than normal, thus avoiding the seasonality of pests, diseases, or weather patterns. Having a crop in the ground for a shorter time means that there are fewer things that can go wrong.

In USDA zone 8 or warmer, I recommend planting fava beans in the fall.

By selecting for frost-tolerant common beans, I have shifted the season forward three to four weeks. The harvest window expands by having an early crop and a main season crop, minimizing the rush to harvest. The earlier harvest matures before the start of the fall monsoons, which can damage the main crop.

Season shifting could be applied to developing varieties that thrive in greenhouses, cold-frames, or near landscape features like boulders, fences, or walls.

Unique Traits

Growing landrace style provides many opportunities to affect the phenotype of the plants or animals. An observant gardener can notice physical traits that are different from other plants. It's likely that the offspring of unique plants carry the unique trait.

As mentioned earlier, in the 1880s, my great-great grandfather noticed one wheat plant in a large field that was growing more robustly and vigorously than the rest. He harvested the seeds separately, and planted them in his home garden. Eventually, his wheat became the most widely planted wheat in northern Utah and southern Idaho.

Decorative tomato flowers

I love the huge, brightly colored flowers in the promiscuous tomato project. I select preferentially for bold floral displays. I daydream about selling tomatoes that are specifically for flower gardens. I expect to select for fruity tasting tomatoes and against regular tomato flavor. Bleck!

The frost tolerant bean project started when about 5% of the young plants survived a late spring frost. I planted the seeds from them the next year, a month early. Many of them survived. I've repeated that for years. The variety is much more frost tolerant than average beans. A survival rate of 5% is great odds when working on adapting plants to local conditions.

Sunroots (Jerusalem artichokes) and annual sunflowers are different species that can cross with each other. Sunroots have large, edible, perennial tubers. Annual sunflowers produce large seeds. Crosses between them are fertile. The selection possibilities are fascinating to me. What if we selected for huge, edible roots and huge seeds on the same plant? What a delightful crop for a permaculture setting.

Sunroots flower very late. To make a cross, I might try planting annual sunflowers every 10 days, to try to get flowering times to line up. Perhaps sunflower pollen can be stored by desiccating and/or freezing. The cotyledons of hybrids are different than either parent.

In the chapter on food security, I discuss the possibilities of perennial sunflowers producing large tubers and lots of large seeds.

In my squash-breeding project, I noticed squash fruits that are fuzzy. They feel super weird. They fascinate me. What if deer really dislike the fuzzy feel and don't eat the fruits? What if the squash bugs can't feed or lay

Fuzzy squash fruits

their eggs because of the fuzz? I'm excited about exploring the possibilities.

My most unique melon grows in what I call bush-style. It has very short inter-nodes. It would be great for someone growing on a balcony, or in raised beds with limited space. I plant it about a hundred feet from my regular muskmelons, to keep the two populations mostly separate.

Bush-type muskmelon

My crops grow in full sunlight in a wide-open field with silty-loam alkaline soil. My crops have self-selected to thrive under those conditions. In other locations, the genetics of the crops might shift to favor shady gardens with acidic, sandy soil. I do not try to change my soil. It is much easier to change the genetics of the plants than it is to make long-term changes to the soil.

I grow perennial wheat and rye. They originated as interspecies hybrids between domesticated grains and wild grasses. Being perennial gives them a big advantage over annual species. It is nice to plant a crop, and know that it will fend for itself without requiring constant attention from a farmer.

One of my favorite fruits is a pear grown from seed. The skin on green fruits is bitter. The bitterness disappears upon ripening. The advantage of bitter skin is that insects won't eat the green fruits. That makes it possible to grow organic pears without crop protection chemicals.

I grow a giant sunflower. It gets 12 feet (4 m) tall. I select for heads that face directly towards the ground. The birds can't hold unto the bottom of the head to eat the seeds. I also select for seeds that are loosely connected to the head, and to each other. That allows me to harvest the seeds in the field, by rubbing a gloved hand over them. I had terrible troubles with mold when I was harvesting whole heads and trying to dry them in cool/damp fall weather. The free-threshing sunflower seeds dry quickly when spread out on a sheet.

Cucumber

Yellow skinned cucumbers showed up in my landrace. The flavor is light and delicate. They are, by far, the best tasting, cucumber that I have encountered. They are wonderful when lacto-fermented or pickled. They are small fruited. I am currently exploring the population to see if fruit size can be increased.

This would be a case where a freelance hybrid with a larger fruited variety could be worthwhile.

Cactus are a family that has a lot of potential for developing new types of crops. Either fruits or leaves may be eaten. Perhaps an edible flower could be developed. I think of the family as more of a species-complex than as discrete species. There are lots of opportunities to discover new and exciting crops among the cactus. For example, some small fruited species don't have

Edible cactus leaves

spines on the fruits! What? Cactus fruits without spines!! That would be a wonderful trait to explore. Perhaps we could select for higher numbers of larger fruits.

Cactus fruits can be really tasty. More than a decade ago, I planted a bunch of Opuntia engelmanii seeds. Most of them winter killed the first winter. Some have survived outside until now. They are among the most flavorful fruits that I eat. They have tiny spines, so I typically eat them by cutting in half, then scooping the insides out with a spoon. A friend burns the spines off with a flame.

Edible cactus fruits

I grow a cultivar of Opuntia humifusa, which is called spineless. It has tiny glochids, but not large spines. I prepare it for eating by rubbing the spines off on the grass of the lawn. I know people that cut off the spine-containing areolas.

A neighbor grows a non-winter-hardy cactus in a large pot, which gets moved inside for the winter. During the summer, she moves it outside, and harvests the young leaves for food.

7 Promiscuous Pollination

Promiscuous pollination is essential to the long term survival of landrace crops. Some species are very promiscuous. Other species are mostly self-pollinating, crossing occasionally.

Promiscuous pollination rearranges the genetics of the plants. Shifting genetics allows life to adapt to changes in the ecosystem or in farming practices.

Highly Localized

Pollination is highly localized. A flower is most likely to be pollinated by the nearest compatible flower. The closer we inter-plant different varieties, the more likely they are to cross. I typically sow the barely crossing varieties jumbled together to get the most crossing possible.

Pollen Flow
(between flowers)

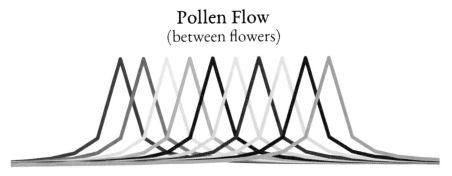

Pollen flow is highly localized

The mathematics of pollination are quadratic, meaning that doubling the distance between two flowers cuts the chances of cross-pollination to a quarter. Increasing the distance tenfold lowers the chances of cross-pollination a hundredfold.

The graph showing pollen flow between flowers applies at any scale. It applies to the separate flowers in the umbel of a carrot as it does between umbels on the same plant. It applies to separate plants in the same patch, and to separate patches in the same field.

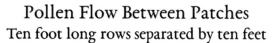

Pollen Flow Between Patches
Ten foot long rows separated by ten feet

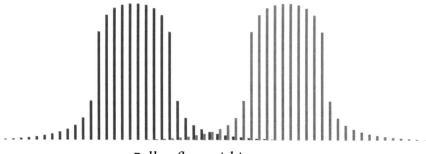

Pollen flow within a row

An awareness of the highly localized nature of pollination allows us to design plantings to either minimize pollination for maintaining isolation distances, or to maximize it to encourage crossing.

Purity and Isolation Distances

People express fear about saving seeds. What if they flub isolation distances? What if a variety gets polluted? How about inbreeding depression? What if the seed is a hybrid? What about poisons and deformed-monster plants? My response is that those things are of little consequence.

The essential knowledge regarding seed saving is that plants produce seeds. They can be harvested and replanted. For plant breeding, add that offspring resemble their parents and grandparents. Sometimes a trait skips a generation.

The Grand Secret of Plant Breeding

Plants make seeds.
Offspring resemble their
parents and grandparents.
Sometimes a trait skips a generation.

Growing landrace populations greatly simplifies seed saving. It reduces worry about plant purity and isolation distances.

Worrying about purity is one of the biggest impediments to seed saving. Maintaining purity leads to inbreeding depression. I don't worry much about isolation distances or keeping cultivars pure. Plants are stronger when cultivars cross-pollinate each other. If a Hubbard squash and a banana squash cross-pollinate, the offspring are still squash. They grow like squash, they look like squash, they cook like squash. When two great varieties cross, the offspring inherit greatness.

People started domesticating plants up to 40,000 years ago. The vast majority of undesirable traits have been eliminated from domesticated crops. I don't observe crossed plants turning into poisonous mutants. When two highly-domesticated varieties cross, the offspring are likewise highly-domesticated. The offspring's traits blend those of the parent varieties.

Sometimes I make crosses to wild, less-domesticated parents. I hope to incorporate more diversity. Occasionally in those crosses, I find a poisonous fruit, or other undesirable traits. Melon, squash, cucumber, bean, and lettuce poisons are well behaved. They taste horrid. Terrible tastes are a good indication that a plant produces poisons. Nightshades might taste good, but the poisons make me want to barf.

I planted a "pocket melon," which is a tiny cantaloupe with a perfume smell. I taste every fruit before saving seeds. The pocket melons tasted nasty! Poison in melons tastes horrid. I discarded the whole year's seed crop. I couldn't risk introducing poison into the cantaloupes.

When I introduced genetics from wild watermelons, the "exploding melon" trait appeared. If jostled while sun-warmed, the fruits popped open. Gradual selection eliminated the trait in a few years.

I consider tepary beans to be semi-domesticated. My original strains had a trait which I call "hard seed." About 10% of the seeds wouldn't absorb water when soaked. They would take weeks or months to germinate. I eliminated that trait by pre-soaking the seeds, and only planting those that absorbed water immediately. The wild watermelon brought the same trait with them, which self-eliminated. Watermelon is a full-season crop at my place. Plants that take a long time to germinate don't reproduce before frost.

These days, if I choose to grow wild ancestors of domesticated crops, I grow them in a separate field for a few years. This ensures that they don't introduce unfortunate traits. It's easier to keep them isolated in the beginning, rather than eliminating a trait later on.

I keep hot peppers separate from sweet peppers. I don't care what a sweet pepper looks like. It can be any shape, any color, or any size as long as it is not hot. The most important sweet pepper trait in my garden is, "must produce fruit."

For the mostly inbreeding crops like common beans and grains, I consider them isolated at 10 feet (3 m) apart. With the mostly outcrossing crops, I consider them isolated at 100 feet (30 m) apart. I observe around 1% to 5% crossing at that distance.

Crops flowering at different times don't cross-pollinate. An early maturing and a late maturing corn may grow next to each other, without worry of crossing. That's how I grow flour corn and sweet corn in the same field.

Likewise, inbreeding depression is only a problem when growing a cultivar in strict isolation. It doesn't much matter how many plants are in the population if new genes arrive regularly. The inflow of new genes is counteracting the gene loss due to inbreeding.

I wonder if the "minimum number of parents" recommendations are a ruse by the mega-seed companies to discourage people from saving seeds. The standards necessary for growing a seed crop for the entire world are much different from what is required for growing local food for the local neighborhood. I'm not going to suggest magic numbers of how many plants to save seeds from. Save seeds from as many as is easy for you and your community. Be generous during selection. If a variety looses vigor, allow it to cross with something else.

I don't care if there are a few percent off-types in what I grow. I'm harvesting by hand. I'm holding each vegetable in my hand before cooking. If I don't like it, I compost it or feed it to animals.

Outcrossing

Cross-pollinating varieties adapt quicker to landrace growing conditions. The frequent rearrangement of genetics allows rapid selection for families that thrive under local conditions.

Corn is wind-pollinated. Corn pollen is heavier than air, and quickly drops to the ground. In my fields with an average wind speed of 10 miles per hour, corn pollen drops below silk level within 25 feet (8 m).

Corn pollen can travel for miles if caught up in the turbulence of a storm. Random grains of foreign pollen have little effect compared to the millions of grains of local pollen. Most corn pollen falls approximately straight down most of the time. When I inadvertently plant a colored corn seed in a patch of white corn, the pollen from the plant with colored kernels colors the kernels on the white cobs. Most of the cross pollination occurs within 3 feet (1 m).

I take advantage of the localized nature of pollination to grow sister lines. I might plant the purple corn together in a block, then the white corn right next to it in a block, then the yellow corn next to the white. At harvest time, the white block will produce primarily white cobs, with a few purple kernels on one edge of the block. A few yellow kernels show up onthe other edge of the block. In this system, there is little crossing between the yellow and the purple. This method allows preservation of different phenotypes.

I plant the green squash on one end of a row, and the orange squash on the other. Then the orange squash mostly pollinate themselves, and the green squash mostly pollinate themselves, maintaining both varieties. Some crossing occurs in the middle of the patch.

Mostly-selfing

The mostly-selfing crops are much more likely to pollinate themselves than to be cross-pollinated. The flowers are shaped in a way that favors self-pollination over crossing. Because of the slow rate of genetic mixing, the mostly selfing crops are slower to adapt to local conditions. Closely inter-planting the mostly-selfing crops encourages crossing.

Imported selfing varieties immediately undergo survival of the fittest selection. Beans are mostly-selfing. Most bean varieties are unsuited for my

Minimal cross-pollination at 3 feet (0.9 m) separation

garden. They fail the first year. I estimate that for every 10 varieties of common beans that I plant, 9 of them don't produce seed to be planted next year. With tomatoes, only about 1 variety in 20 produces ripe fruit before the plants are killed by fall frosts. In later years, beans and tomatoes get along adequately as inbreeding varieties in a mix of other inbreeding varieties.

The natural cross-pollination rate of domesticated common beans is between 0.5 to 5%. That is sufficient for natural selection. Watching for the naturally-occurring hybrids and planting them preferentially can speed up local adaptation.

Even without intentional selection for crossed beans, the offspring of crosses will tend to be more productive, and will thus create more seeds than the inbreeding varieties. The population will inadvertently shift to favor the varieties that are more outcrossing.

Making manual crosses mixes up the genetics of mostly-selfing crops. For the next two to four generations, the mixed-up genes rearrange themselves into new combinations. Some of those combinations may be well adapted to current growing conditions. My tepary bean landrace really thrived after Andy Breuninger sent manually produced tepary hybrids. He did the crosses on a small scale. A few hybrid seeds dramatically increased the seed-coat colors of my tepary beans.

Maintaining a healthy ecosystem in the garden and surrounding areas increases cross-pollination due to more pollinators. Pollinator populations are healthier when many species of plants are feeding them through their entire life cycle.

I welcome all species of plants to my farm and the surrounding wildlands. I call them "native" as soon as they become established. When I look at plants with my own eyes, I can't tell when or where they originated. I observe all plants providing abundant ecosystem services, such as biomass, pollen, nectar, and shelter.

Tepary, before making hybrids

Tepary, after making hybrids

8 Food Security

Community

The ultimate food security comes from living in a cooperative community. The more we localize our food resources within a community, the more secure we make them. Maintaining a local food and seed network provides security from global and regional disruptions to the food supply.

The fewer intermediaries that exist between food production and food consumption, the more secure the food system becomes. The most secure food system is one in which every member of the community contributes in some way to the food production of the community.

The contribution might be buying food at the farmer's market, or allowing a gardener to grow food on a vacant lot. It might be making kimchi or pickles from local produce. The doctor's office could grow tomatoes instead of inedible shrubs.

My local food cooperative provides social benefits to feed my soul: touching, singing, dancing, drumming, celebrating. One of the sweetest things is sharing food at the annual planting celebration that was grown on the farm last summer. This food was grown from seeds, planted during the previous planting celebration.

I grow many species and types of food. Much of the food I eat is local food that I didn't produce myself. I feed the community vegetables. They feed me other types of foods.

I don't bake. I gift food to the local bakery. They give me bread. I gift honey to a hunter. He gifts me venison. A fisherman gives me fish.

When a relationship went haywire, and I lost seeds, my local and Internet communities gave them back to me.

Inbreeding vs. Diversity

The recent history of agriculture demonstrates crop failures due to a pest overcoming a plant's defenses, then spreading widely in a short period of time. This wildfire-like spread of pathogens is due to genetic uniformity in the affected crops. Similar failures happen due to weather. Landrace gardening avoids these problems by maintaining wide genetic diversity within and between species.

After the 1970 corn blight, the National Academy of Sciences warned that crops in the United States are "impressively vulnerable" to failure due to genetic uniformity. The trend toward uniformity accelerated since that time. I expect the trend to continue in mega-agriculture due to the increasing mechanization of farming.

A counter-trend is occurring among small scale growers. The reasons given for seeking out genetically diverse crops varies among gardeners. Some are seeking a wider flavor palate. Others love the exciting colors. Some want higher nutritional content.

I grow landrace crops primarily for their reliability: The plants are less susceptible to total crop failure. I reap the benefit of my food not looking or tasting bland and boring. I harvest by hand. I do not benefit from uniformity.

Cloning

Crops grown by cloning are particularly susceptible to massive crop failure. A pest that overcomes the defenses of one clone can over-run the entire population. I avoid growing clones in favor of promiscuously pollinated crops. I expand the biodiversity of crops in my garden, by growing traditionally cloned crops from seeds, instead of cloning.

Potatoes

Most commercial potato varieties are sterile clones. They are unable to produce seeds. I trialed many varieties to find some that produce viable seeds. I stopped growing non-fruiting varieties. By growing potatoes from promiscuously pollinated seeds, I minimize the risk of a potato famine affecting my valley. Those of us involved in this endeavor say that we are growing "true potato seed." William Whitson of Cultivariable is a wonderful resource for obtaining true potato seeds.

Sunroots

Sunroots are a food security crop for me. They grow like weeds. They thrive in my ecosystem. The soil here is like the silty loam of their natural habitat (just drier than where cattails grow). I harvest a few bushels of sunroots per year for eating and sharing with seed-keepers. Most of them stay in the ground.

Sunroots store well in the ground. I can harvest them between October and April, whenever the ground isn't frozen. I've never caught anyone stealing sunroots. They are hard to dig, and most people don't recognize them as food. Sunroots are a hill people crop, producing food year after year, even if it doesn't get harvested in any particular year.

I grow genetically diverse sunroots from seeds. Sunroots are typically grown as clones, which are self-incompatible, and thus do not set seeds. My sunroots set seed prolifically because unrelated individuals promiscuously pollinate each other.

Largest 15% of wild sunroots

I crossed a domestic sunroot with a wild strain from Kansas. I re-selected for great tubers. The domestic strain is knobby. It is hard to use in the kitchen. Dirt gets embedded between the knobs. I selected for large non-knobby tubers.

A cross-pollinating crop can adapt to my garden. I grew about 50 sunroot seedlings per year for three generations. Selecting each generation for the best growing clones. They promiscuously cross-pollinated each other prior to the next generation.

Each year, I saved around 15% of the new varieties. I now grow them as clones. A clone is always a clone. My sunroot clones are better suited to my ecosystem and culinary needs than commercially available clones. I could restart the breeding project at any time. Because I grow a promiscuously pollinating population, new seeds form each year. Some of them may be sprouting and creating new cultivars.

Goldfinches love sunroot seeds. To collect large numbers of seeds, I either harvest shortly after petal-drop, or put a mesh bag over the seed-heads.

We cook sunroots by adding small amounts to soups, roasts, and stir-fries. They have a reputation for being gassy to people that are not used to eating probiotically. Small doses helps to avoid flatulence. We boil sunroots in milk and blend to make a soup. We lacto-ferment them.

Garlic

The garlic genome has suffered even more than potatoes from monoculture cloning. Most clones are incapable of making seeds.

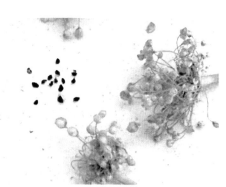

True garlic seeds

We obtained wild ancestors from the Tian Shan Mountains in Central Asia. They have retained the ability to make seeds. We are creating new clones for immediate use. Longer term this project may produce a landrace of promiscuously pollinated garlic. We say that we are growing "true garlic seed."

Garlic has both bulbils and seed pods in the umbel. The bulbils tend to grow tightly together and crush the flower stems. To avoid this, we remove the bulbils just after the flowers open. Some varieties have bulbils that are loosely connected. Other bulbils firmly adhere. I select for bulbils that fall out easily when jostled. Some plants can make seeds successfully without removing bulbils.

The purple striped varieties are the most closely related to ancestral garlic, and have been most useful.

Planting garlic via the winter-sown method has been most reliable. Some seeds sprout without cold treatment. I favor those varieties. Long-term, I want to plant garlic as a spring sown annual, just like onions.

Germination of first generation garlic seeds can be around 5%. By growing from seeds generation after generation, we are selecting for varieties that produce seed more readily.

Avram Drucker of Garlicana is a wonderful resource for acquiring garlic varieties that are able to produce true seed.

Trees

Cloning trees is common. That is advantageous because of brand recognition, and consistency. It is dangerous from a food security standpoint. It risks system wide crop failure, due to a pest overcoming defense mechanisms. Arabica coffee, and Cavendish banana are tree crops with worldwide distribution that are threatened by imminent system-wide failure. They are examples of the dangers of basing a food system on cloning.

For maximum food security, I recommend growing food-producing trees from seed. That allows local adaptation. It affords resilience to pests and disease. Later in the book I devote a subsection to discussing seed-grown trees.

Full-Season Growing

Growing different species allows harvest at different times of year. Growing food in all seasons enhances food security. Growing different types of crops allows different storage methods. Squash store on a dry shelf at room temperature. Root crops store best in cool, damp, dark places. Spring greens are great foraged hand to mouth outdoors.

One of my neighbors plants spinach in mid-August. It overwinters as young plants. In the spring, it is ready to eat before anyone else has even thought about planting seeds.

Mushrooms

Mushrooms are wonderful for adding diversity to a homestead. They typically fruit during periods of heavy rainfall. The garden is way too muddy at those times for working. Mushroom foraging time!

I only grow mushrooms outdoors. I'm not willing to try to sterilize everything for an indoor grow. I worked decades as a chemist. Sterilization is unsatisfactory to me. I don't like it emotionally nor philosophically. And it's way too much work.

My basic method is to blend any cast-off mushroom pieces in the water used to wash them. Dump the slurry on suitable growing materials.

Mushrooms fend for themselves, when planted into appropriate habitats. Harvest involves checking on them during or immediately after damp weather.

There is a section on growing mushrooms later in the book.

Spring Greens

I grow skirret. It is a perennial, and is my earliest harvest of greens in the spring. During the summer and fall, I don't care for its taste. After a winter of being deprived of greens, skirret is a special treat. To me, dandelions are edible only if picked from plants grown in the shade before any hint of hot weather.

Egyptian onions are ready to harvest two weeks after the snow melts. They are a soul-satisfying food first thing in the spring. I eat them all summer as green onions. Under my growing conditions, they offer scallions during the entire growing season.

Kale, cabbage, or Brussels sprouts may overwinter. The greens produced in early spring are the sweetest of the year.

Root Crops

Overwintered in ground

I grow sunroots, carrots, and turnips that stay in the ground during the winter. It's comforting to know that I can dig them whenever the ground isn't frozen. I may put straw over them in the fall to minimize freezing.

Root cellars store crops that do best in dark, damp conditions. My grandpa's root cellar was a hole in the ground that held a few buckets of potatoes. He covered it with a board and straw.

Seeds

Seed saving generates many more seeds than required for planting. Many types of seeds are edible either by themselves, or added to bread, stir-fry, or soup.

Spice blenders can convert seeds into edible flours. Freshly prepared mustard spice is awesome.

Multi-species Diversity

In addition to maintaining biodiversity within a species, we can increase the diversity and reliability of our gardens by growing additional species. Instead of growing only common beans, I grow fava, garden pea, winter pea, runner bean, Lupini, tepary, cowpea, garbanzo, lima bean, lentil, fenugreek, alfalfa, and grasspea. It is unlikely for a disease, parasite, weed, insect or weather pattern to overcome all species at the same time.

Some legumes like hot/humid weather. Some thrive in hot/dry weather. Some are frost tolerant or winter hardy. With many preferences between them, some variety or other is likely to thrive, regardless of the weather.

I might not prefer the taste of some alternate species. In a survival situation, I would eat them, and love them. The fig-leaved gourd has white flesh, and seeds arranged like in a watermelon. It is bland tasting. It seems impervious to squash bugs and diseases. Its seeds are large and edible.

Foraging

Grain, mushrooms, trees, and medicinal herbs are species that may be planted into the wildlands and harvested as needed. Many wildland species are useful for food. Taking advantage of them as a food source is as easy as paying attention to what grows where and when, then checking on them at appropriate times. I love making up harvest memes for myself like the following.

- Check for morels when the grass is 6" tall.
- Check the apricot grove on Bryce's birthday.
- It's been two weeks since the snow melted, pick onions.
- It rained two days ago. Check for oyster mushrooms.

Weeds are important for food security. They are more locally adapted than anything that can be purchased from far away. I eat more wild lambs quarters than lettuce. I eat more wild-crafted oyster mushrooms than store-bought button mushrooms.

Seed Swap

Ogden Seed Exchange

Saturday
Feb 9th, 2019
10:00 AM - Noon

Ogden Preparatory Academy
1415 Lincoln Ave. - Ogden

NOTE- Begining this year only locally grown and saved seeds will be welcome at this event.

You do not have to bring your own seeds to participate and remember to bring envelopes or baggies for your trade or purchase.

For questions email us : ogdenseedexchange@gmail.com
Visit Ogden Seed Exchange on Facebook

Supported By:

Delectation of Tomatoes, etc.
www.delectationoftomatoes.com

Joseph Lofthouse
Landrace Seedsman

9 Landrace Maintenance

Landraces are most easily maintained as a community effort. The best and strongest landrace crops are those which are widely grown throughout a local or regional community.

I frequently swap seeds with the neighbors. This lets me take advantage of the localization that they have done to our valley. I know the practices of some neighbors better than others. Some neighbors have been long-term collaborators and I trust their seed completely and plant it in large quantity. I know nothing of other neighbors. I treat their seed as foreign seed and plant in limited quantities, or in semi-isolation.

The Ogden Seed Exchange is my most important venue for sharing and acquiring locally-adapted seeds. The swap has a policy of "local seeds only."

I consider it my duty as a farmer to maintain healthy and thriving landrace populations for the crops that are most desired by the people that I feed. My protocol for doing so is:

- Swap seeds with the neighbors.
- Occasionally add new genetics.
- Plant some older seed each year.
- Grow large enough populations to maintain diversity.
- Be liberal during selection.
- Give priority to naturally occurring hybrids.

Add New Genetics

I add a small amount of new varieties to my landrace vegetables from time to time. I call them foreign varieties because they are not from this area. There might be something in the new material that is just what my garden needs. If they do well, I may save seeds from them. If they do poorly, they may contribute pollen. I plant up to 10 percent non-locally adapted seed each year without worry about it dramatically affecting my landraces.

The constant inflow of new genetics minimizes inbreeding depression. It keeps the effective population size higher. It may bring in useful genes.

Keep Older Genetics

Each year I include seeds from several previous years in my plantings. I do this to avoid having the genetic balance of the population shifted radically by a single odd growing season. That helps to retain plants that do well in hotter or cooler growing seasons, and in wetter or drier seasons. This seed contributes about 10 to 30 percent of my crop.

Prefer Larger Populations

Best practice for seed saving and plant breeding is to maintain larger populations to avoid inbreeding depression. I'm not going to specify population sizes. Just don't replant one seed for generation after generation.

Historically, large populations were maintained by sharing seeds as a community. The population size equals the population of all the plants grown in all the gardens in the community. Planting seeds from several previous generations increases the total population size. Combining seed from small gardens and large gardens increases the total population size.

I don't worry about population size in crops that are highly diverse. It's mostly a problem in outcrossing varieties that are already inbred.

Loss of vigor isn't as noticeable in the species that are mostly selfing. We are comparing them to their peers that are already suffering from inbreeding depression.

I love growing hybrid beans. They are vigorous and robust. For a few generations they are the most vigorous in the garden. Then they revert to the baseline inbreeding and lose vigor.

The seed saving literature is filled with rules about growing large populations of plants to avoid inbreeding. Those recommendations are geared towards crops that have been highly inbred for 8 to 50 generations. The high diversity within landrace crops minimizes the risk of inbreeding depression.

Gardeners with limited space can grow vigorous seed, in limited space, by following the guidelines in this chapter.

A technique that I use for maintaining high populations in limited space is to crowd plantings. For example, I plant 10 to 25 tomato plants into one clump. Or I plant a row of tomatoes spaced six inches (15 cm) apart.

Select Liberally

Selecting liberally means saving seeds from plants with various sizes, shapes, colors, textures, flavors and maturity dates. I save lots of seed from great-growing plants, and less seed from plants that struggle. I save more seed from plants that produce great-tasting food than from plants that are less flavorful. If the food is edible, it's a candidate for seed saving. This allows the population to become localized while preserving genetic diversity. Diversity allows the seed to adapt to changing climate, bugs, soil, and practices of the farmer.

Prioritize Crossing

If I notice a naturally occurring hybrid among a typically selfing species, I save that seed separately. It gets a special place in next year's garden. I treasure the rare hybrids, because they are vigorous. They have unique genetics that might thrive in my garden.

By saving seeds from naturally crossed plants, I select for offspring that are more likely to cross. Perhaps the flowers were slightly more open. Perhaps they had a smell or a color that was more attractive to pollinators. Offspring resemble their parents and grandparents; therefore preferentially planting crossed seeds moves the population towards higher crossing rates.

Summary

These practices maintain a large genetic base for landrace crops, and help to avoid inbreeding depression. The population size of a landrace maintained in this way includes all the plants grown in all the gardens, over all the years. This protocol allows for the preservation of existing landraces while allowing them to continuously adapt to local conditions.

Genetically diverse seed is more likely to survive into the far future. Adding new genetics from time to time increases genetic diversity. Being liberal in selection and planting seed from previous years helps to maintain local adaptation and a larger population size. Saving crossed seed helps the population adapt to changing conditions. Sharing within a community helps mitigate personal foibles and melt-downs.

10 Pests and Diseases

I welcome pests and diseases in my garden. Because they guide my plants to become strong and resilient, I welcome all species of plants, animals, fungi, and micro-organisms. They bring me joy.

I don't try to kill bugs, or eradicate diseases. I may even aid their survival. I don't spray poisons on my garden. I don't spray with substitutes for poisons. I want my plants to be fully compatible with the existing ecosystem. Therefore, my plants live or die without intervention from me. I don't often pay attention to pests or diseases. If I'm getting a harvest of tasty produce, I don't fuss with the details.

If I were to try to kill any specific type of pest or microbe, I would inadvertently be damaging all of them, including those that provide essential symbiotic benefits to the plants.

This attitude saves me time, money, and stress. The initial cost savings are obvious. I'm not spending money to buy inputs, nor the labor to apply them. Less obvious are the long-term benefits. By allowing my plants to co-exist with weeds, bugs, diseases, and microbes, the plants are self-selecting for varieties that thrive in their presence.

Return To Resistance

I highly recommend Raoul Robinson's *Return to Resistance: Breeding Crops to Reduce Pesticide Dependence*. It is freely available for download as a PDF. The way I remember his advice is that he advocates growing crops in areas filled with diseases and pests. Although it may seem counter-intuitive, cull the plants that thrive, keeping only those that seem to be highly susceptible to pests or diseases, then select among the survivors in succeeding years for those that do well.

His method selects for plants that have many genes that each add a little resistance. This is called horizontal resistance. Each gene has only a small effect on the overall health of the plant. If a pest or disease overcomes one gene, the plant still has many others that contribute to overall resistance.

When a single gene has a huge impact on resistance (as may be the case with the initial thriving plants that were culled), this is called vertical resistance. Plants that rely on vertical resistance for survival are susceptible to sudden system-wide failure.

It's common in seed catalogs, especially with tomatoes, to have lists of resistance genes that the plant carries, for example: VFNTA. People think that the more of these genes a plant carries, the more resistance it has.

I've reached a different conclusion after reading Raoul's work, and paying attention to my own garden.

Single gene resistances are susceptible to failure, leading to system wide failure due to the resistance depending on that one gene. In the promiscuously pollinating tomato project, we intentionally chose to start with older varieties that are not known to have named resistance genes. Because they are 100% outcrossing, they re-shuffle genes rapidly, to re-combine many genes with small effect into highly-resistant plants.

Colorado Potato Beetle

Colorado potato beetles don't bother my potatoes even though beetles and potatoes are both common in my garden. The beetles live in my garden all year. That means that I can make a multi-year contract with them. I can influence both their genetics and their culture.

My contract with the beetles goes something like this:

- I will never apply a poison to my garden, nor harass any beetle abiding by the contract.
- The beetles may eat the wild Solanum physalifolium that grows as a weed in my garden. I will not harm beetles that only eat weeds.
- I will allow the weed to grow in some areas of the garden.
- Beetles found on a vegetable get crushed.
- Any domesticated plant that repeatedly attracts beetles gets culled.

That's pretty much the contract. The beetles eat the weeds. They leave the vegetables alone. This strategy would not work with insects that blow in on the wind. It works with year round residents.

A mother beetle tends to lay her eggs on the same species of plant that she hatched on. This is the beetle culture that I mentioned. Baby beetles grow up and do what they learned from their mother. There may be a self-reinforcing genetic component as well, because the beetles come to prefer to eat solanum weeds. Those that eat vegetables are less likely to reproduce.

Sometimes, a specific tomato or potato plant gets infested repeatedly. The beetles that are doing the infesting and the vegetable plant are both killed. I don't want to grow vegetables that are producing smells or textures that confuse the beetles, muddying the terms of the contract. I don't want to raise a generation of beetles that finds domestic plants attractive. I do animal breeding on the beetles, and plant breeding on the vegetables, encouraging them to peacefully co-exist.

Birds and Mammals

The first year I grew Astronomy Domine sweet corn, it had wide variation of phenotypes. Some plants grew waist high, so the cobs were at a perfect height for pheasants to eat the cobs. I saved seeds only from the taller plants. In later generations, pheasants did not bother the corn crop.

A few years later, raccoons and skunks started preying on a different variety of corn. I allowed them to have what they wanted. I saved seeds from cobs that the critters didn't eat. After a few years, the stalks were stiffer. The cobs grew higher off the ground. Predation by mammals was no longer a problem.

The plants solved their own problems with birds and mammals. I thought about what I was harvesting for seed. If a plant was laying flat on the ground, and the animals had only eaten the top half of the kernels, I didn't save seeds from it. I only saved seeds from cobs on tall, strong plants, that the animals hadn't eaten.

An inadvertent side-effect of the anti-predator selection, was that the cobs are now much higher off the ground. They are about chest high, which makes harvesting easier. I don't like stooping over to harvest.

Fuzz

Fuzzy leaves or fruits may deter predation by insects or mammals, so I'm exploring fuzziness on several species. With fewer insect bites, fewer microbes and viruses end up in the plant. Perhaps fuzz reduces sun-scald on fruits, especially in the desert, or at high altitude.

Harvesting fuzzy fruits might mean wearing gloves while harvesting. I already do that for okra. I'd be OK doing it with other crops.

If I end up selecting for fuzzy tomato fruits, they might be canning tomatoes only. I don't like the feel of fuzz on my tongue. It wouldn't matter on winter squash, because I usually don't eat winter squash skin.

Blossom End Rot

I read about people's travails with blossom end rot. They blame themselves for providing the wrong soil, or inconsistent watering. They use elaborate fertilizing protocols, and exotic ingredients to try to avoid rotting fruit.

My tomatoes and squash are not bothered by blossom end rot. That is because I do not tolerate it in my garden. If a plant has even one fruit with blossom end rot, the entire plant gets culled as soon as I notice. My garden is a no-excuses zone.

My attitude towards blossom end rot, is that it's not a soil problem, or a watering issue. It's not due to negligence by the gardener. I attribute blossom end rot to a genetic predisposition in the plant. It is trivial to select for plants that are not prone to blossom end rot.

If you save seeds from plants that had blossom end rot, you are selecting for the continuation of that trait. Do yourself and future generations a favor, and stop growing and saving seeds from varieties that are prone to blossom end rot. We don't need to be curating old tomato varieties with maladapted traits.

Moths and Butterflies

I welcome life into my garden. All species are welcome to live among my crops. Moths and butterflies bring me joy. I'm delighted to provide for them. People badmouth the caterpillars of tomato horn-worms, because they eat tomato leaves. They grow huge, and eat a lot! I read about people waging battle on the caterpillars for the sake of a few extra tomato fruits. I am glad to share the tomatoes with the hummingbird moths. My crops grow abundantly. There are plenty of tomatoes to share. The caterpillars turn into hummingbird moths, which have a special place in my heart, because I watched them often while laying near grandmother's flower beds. My heart sings when I see them.

Sometimes, the caterpillars host parasitic wasps, which is good for my ecosystem, and for reducing insect populations. The hummingbird moths have extra-long tongues, which can pollinate crops, that other pollinators can't reach. My local ecosystem is healthier because I allow the tomato hornworms to co-exist with my garden. I provide nesting sites for the parasitic wasps.

Hummingbird moth

Likewise, I welcome the cabbage moths and their caterpillars. I maintain an intact ecosystem, and therefore, their numbers are moderate. I grow red cabbage and kale, because the green caterpillars are more visible to predators, which keep their numbers in check naturally.

In my ecosystem, cabbage moths blow in with the summer monsoonal rains. Overwintering brassicas such as winter hardy kale and Brussels sprouts are harvested before the moths arrive. Some spring-planted brassica species are harvested before the moths arrive. Other species are not favored by the moths.

I allow showy milkweed as a weed in my fields. It feeds perhaps a hundred Monarch butterflies each summer. If a milkweed plant is growing in a row, I allow it to grow, perhaps even sacrificing the nearest vegetables to give it space.

Micro-organisms

I treat the microbiome in my body and fields as a precious resource. I avoid bringing substances into field or body that might damage the microbial life that lives within me and my fields. Each species plays a vital role in the dance of life. It would be foolish of me to eradicate portions of the microbiome without knowing what role they play.

The longer I garden, the clearer it becomes, that I ought to also be sharing a sample of the soil in which the species grew, in order to transfer as much of an intact ecosystem as possible. My plants are intimately and synergistically connected to the microbiome of my farm and body. Sucking on seeds before planting them is a great way to return a portion of that microbiome to the field.

Lofthouse Landrace Moscha 2020 · Bokchoi GRE · Big-leaf Tobacco 2015 · Opuntia humifusa 2013/6 · Jaoadka 2020

Acorn Delicata 2019 · Small Manli 2017B · fig leaf gourd 2018 · Tomato · Mosperaia 2018 · Lofthouse heritage wheat since 1890 · Tepary 2020

High Carotene Sweet 2020 · Winter pea · Maxima Landrace · Fava 2020 · Winter Hardy Kale 2017 · Dry Bush 2020

Lofthouse Flour corn 2019 · Bloodnick mort 2019 · Paradise Se 2019

11 Saving Seeds

Seed saving is an integral part of landrace gardening. We can localize our gardens to our specific growing conditions and way of doing things by planting genetically diverse seed, allowing them to cross-pollinate, and then saving and replanting the seeds.

Saving seeds doesn't have to be the complicated, highly involved, and technical process that some writers advocate. Before the invention of writing, illiterate people were saving seeds. They developed our most popular food crops. Plant seeds are resilient. It doesn't much matter what specific techniques we use while saving seeds. We don't have to clean our seeds like robots do. Our seeds are likely to grow when planted. The important thing about landrace gardening is to be saving and replanting localized, genetically-diverse seeds.

The essential knowledge regarding seed saving is that plants produce seeds, and that seeds can be planted to grow a new plant. It's also good to know that offspring resemble their parents and grandparents, and that sometimes a trait skips a generation. We may not know who the father is. We can know who the mother is. Siblings tend to have similar traits, whether they are full siblings or half siblings.

As a landrace gardener, I don't worry much about plant purity. A dry soup bean is a dry soup bean, regardless of color, size, or species.

People say that home gardeners shouldn't save seeds because they might not breed true. To me, that is a great reason to save seeds. I don't want clones of the mother plant. I want to grow a genetically-diverse, cross-pollinating family, so that the offspring can become localized to my garden. Saving seeds as a landrace gardener alleviates the isolation issues that are difficult for people that are trying to maintain purity in highly inbred cultivars. I want my plants to be cross-pollinating.

Humans are social creatures. We thrive by sharing and cooperating with each other. Even if I don't grow every species of seed that I need for my farm, I have developed a collaboration network of nearby growers. We share seeds among ourselves. I love my seed sharing network, because while the seed might not be exactly tailored to my garden, it is well adapted to my valley. If my local network doesn't have genetically diverse landrace seed, my collaborators from further away may contribute genetic diversity.

Harvesting Seeds

There are two main ways to harvest seeds. The seeds are in dry plant material, or they are inside wet fruits.

Dry harvesting

For dry plant material, harvesting generally consists of crushing the plant material, then separating the seeds from the chaff through screening and/or winnowing. This works best on completely dry plants.

If seeds are falling out before the plant is dry, I pick the plants and store them on a tarp away from rain and dew. After they dry, then I thresh and winnow.

The seeds that are dry-harvested are safe in a short rainstorm. If the forecast is for weeks of rain, I might harvest them before the storm, and store them in a dry airy place until threshing. Moisture and mold are not a friend of dry-harvested seeds.

Some seeds rest in cup-like pods. Poppies are an example. Harvesting them is as easy as tipping the pod upside down over a container. No point crushing the seed pod if the seeds are more cleanly harvested by an easier technique.

Some seed pods crush easily by stepping on them. Other seed pods require more force, such as beating with a stick. I really like pulling the plants, and hitting them against the inside of a garbage can until the seeds fall out. I use this technique for crops like beans, lettuce, mustard, kale, flax.

Seeds remain in the chaff after screening. Great uses for these materials are feeding animals, or seeding sections of garden or the wildlands.

Seeds that we are saving ourselves don't have to look as pristine as commercial seeds. They still grow great, even if we plant some chaff with the seeds.

I avoid harvesting weed seeds with my vegetable seeds. If I don't harvest weed seeds, then I don't have to deal with them later. Screens can be really effective at separating vegetable seeds from weed seeds. Winnowing technique can also be an effective separation strategy. Fox-tail grass seed is easily separated from dry bush beans by either screening or winnowing.

Dirt is hard to separate from seeds. I like to use shears to cut off the plants just above ground level, to avoid including dirt with the seeds.

Wet harvesting

Wet harvest of seeds often happens simultaneously with eating a fruit.

Fermenting is common for wet seeds in fruits, because they have protective membranes that need to rot away before the seed can germinate. Extract the seeds, and allow them to rot for zero to five days, then use flotation or colanders, to separate the seeds from the pulp.

My technique for tomatoes is to cut the bottom of the fruit near the blossom end, then squeeze the juice into a container. Let the container sit for about three days, more or less, depending on temperature. The seeds are ready for further processing when the gel-sack around the seed disintegrates. Add water to the container. The pulp floats. The seeds sink. Rinsing a few times separates the seeds from the pulp. Cucumbers also have a gel coat around the seeds, which disintegrates after a few days of fermentation.

Cantaloupes and watermelons do not have much of a gel coat. Seeds can be harvested and immediately rinsed in a colander until clean. Some squash seeds have a gel coat around them, but I generally don't ferment squash seeds, because the gel coat dries up and blows away during winnowing. I separate the seeds from the pulp with a jet of water against seeds contained in a colander.

Spread the seeds out to dry. Dry seeds thoroughly and quickly to avoid mold.

Winnow to separate good seeds from empty seed coats.

Seed Viability

Seeds reach viability long before full maturity. Immature fruits often contain viable seeds. They might not grow as vigorously as fully mature seeds, but they grow. In my first few years of trying to grow muskmelons and moschata squash, the fruits were very immature. Seeds may continue to mature inside a fruit, even though it has been picked.

Seed viability can be severely harmed if the seed freezes while wet. I harvest wet seed crops before hard freezes. Fully dried seeds of temperate species can be frozen without damage.

Mold or moisture reduce seed viability. I spread seeds out after harvest to dry quickly and thoroughly without molding.

Storing Seeds

If we are saving seeds, it seems important to store them well.

The general wisdom regarding seed storage is cool, dark, and dry. I interpret cool to mean room temperature, and dark to mean not in direct sunlight.

```
Seed Storage

Cool
Dark
Dry
Safe
```

A great seed storage strategy should take into account the typical ways that seeds get lost. In my personal experience, seeds are most commonly lost or damaged in the following ways: human foibles, animals, bugs, moisture, heat, decay and disasters.

Human Foibles

The most common way that seeds disappear is due to human foibles. Grandpa dies and the people cleaning the house throw away precious family heirlooms. People get divorced and the non-gardening spouse takes the seed stash. Seeds get misplaced. They get left in the back of the truck during a rainstorm. Thieves steal. Things get dropped or broken. The rent doesn't get paid on a storage unit.

One of the best ways, to avoid losing seeds to human foibles, is to live a life of peaceful cooperation with others. I have lost treasured varieties due to absent-mindedness, crop failure, and mice. When my collaborators find out they say things like "You gave that variety to me five years ago. I love it! I've sent you a packet of seed."

I keep archive copies of my garden seeds at the homes of friends and relatives. If something bad happens to my main seed supply, I still have backup seeds. I send archive copies of my seeds to collaborators. They can stash the seeds, or plant them, or donate them away. More than a few times I've had seeds come back to me from the collaborator's stashes.

Animals

Twice in my life, mice have gotten into my seed stash and eaten nearly every seed. Both occasions occurred after I moved and a box of seeds got left in the garage. The mice chewed into plastic totes and cardboard boxes and ate the entire seed stash except for one bottle of seeds stored in a glass mason jar.

Now, my preferred storage method for seeds is glass jars with steel lids. I use sizes from four ounces (0.15 kg) to one gallon.

For larger quantities, I use five-gallon (19 l) plastic buckets with screw on lids.

Once in a while, I drop a bottle of seeds in the field, and it breaks. These days, I tend to transfer the amount of seeds I want to plant into a plastic bag and return the excess to the glass jar when I get home. I stuff lots of small packets of seed into wide-mouthed jars.

Bugs

Bugs are the next most common way that I lose seeds. They likewise chew through plastic, paper, and cardboard. They sneak through tiny little cracks. I often can't tell by looking at a packet of seeds if it contains bugs. There are lots of different species of bugs that attack seeds. Some get into my seed stash as eggs that are harvested with the seed. Others arrive during processing or storage.

Freezing kills bugs. The seed should be dry and ready for storage before freezing. Freezing damp seed may damage the embryo. A couple of days in a home freezer is sufficient. Freeze in a hermetically-sealed waterproof container (plastic bag or glass jar), to prevent absorption of moisture after removing from the freezer.

I have run germination tests on dry seeds both before and after freezing. I haven't observed detrimental effects on the temperate varieties that I've tested. Freezing may damage tropical seeds.

Vigorously shaking a bottle of seeds mechanically crushes bugs and eggs. I shake seeds both before and after freezing.

I protect from reinfection by storing in glass jars.

Seed-eating bugs arrive in my home from the grocery store. I do not allow infestations to continue. A thorough cleaning of the pantry occurs whenever I notice bugs. If I keep the population of bugs low, then they are less likely to eat my seeds. I freeze incoming grain products to reduce the number of bugs arriving from the grocery store. Incoming seeds are frozen before being put in the seed stash.

Spiders are welcome to live year round in the seed room.

Moisture

Excess moisture during storage reduces a seed's life-expectancy, or encourages growth of microorganisms. I use a couple of seat-of-the-pants methods to estimate how dry seeds are. I'll do a bite test. If the seed is still soft enough to bite, then it is too moist to store. Another test I use is to put a glass jar or plastic bag of seeds outside in the sunlight. If moisture beads up on the inside of the container then they are too moist.

In my super-arid climate, seeds readily dry to low moisture. People that live in damper climates may need to take active steps to dry seeds. I like using a dehydrator set at 95 °F (35 °C). I also dry seeds by spreading them out on a tarp or cookie sheet.

Desiccants can reduce the moisture in seeds. I like using white rice because it is readily available: Dry the rice in the oven at 225 °F (107 °C) for about four hours. Cool. Place in airtight container such as a gallon sized glass jar. Add seeds in paper or fabric envelopes. Dry for about a week. A collaborator reports that she gets similar results with lichens.

Commercial seeds that are sold in paper envelopes typically have too much moisture for optimal storage. I recommend drying them before storage. They can be dried paper envelope and all.

Once dry, protect the seeds from atmospheric moisture.

In my writings, I focus on the northern varieties which I grow. Seeds of tropical species may not respond well to dehydration.

Heat

Most species of dry seeds store well at room temperature. The physical chemistry of biological systems roughly operates on the principle that for every 18 °F (10 °C) increase in temperature, the rate of reaction doubles. So a variety of seed that is expected to last eight years at 70 °F (21 °C) would only be expected to survive four years at 88 °F (31 °C), two years at 106 °F (41 °C), and one year at

124 °F (51 °C). Given a choice between storing seeds in a hot place or a cool place, choose the cooler location.

Decay

In like manner, for every decrease in temperature of 18 °F (10 °C) the rate of reaction is cut in half. Seeds expected to be viable for 8 years at room temperature, would survive for 32 years in the refrigerator or 128 years in the freezer. If dry, freezing seeds puts their life-expectancy on hold. When removed from freezing temperatures, their biological decay starts up again.

Disasters

I have not lost seeds to disasters. Nevertheless, I plan for them. I keep seed stashes in three different counties. One stash is susceptible to flood, wildfire, and theft. Two stashes are immune from flood but susceptible to earthquake. All stashes are susceptible to fire. By spreading the seeds out, I mitigate against them being destroyed at the same time. The shelves of my primary seed bank bolt to the wall, and have a lip around them to protect from earthquake. They are in glass jars. If I wanted an extra measure of security, I could put plastic bags inside the jars so that even if the jars break the seeds would be contained. People in other areas should include plans for getting their seeds through their most likely disasters: For example, burying seeds in Tornado Alley.

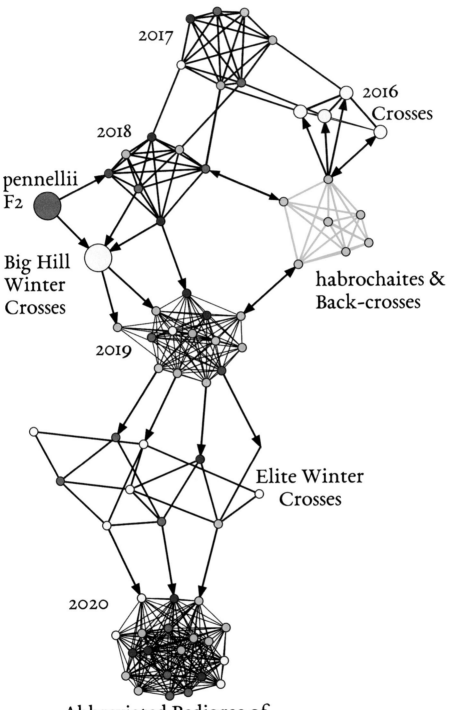

2017

2016 Crosses

2018

pennellii F2

Big Hill Winter Crosses

habrochaites & Back-crosses

2019

Elite Winter Crosses

2020

Abbreviated Pedigree of the Beautifully Promiscuous & Tasty Tomato Project

12 Promiscuous Tomatoes

The Beautifully Promiscuous and Tasty Tomato Project aims to create a population of great-tasting self-incompatible tomatoes. The plausible promise of the project is that the tomatoes will retain marvelous genetic diversity from the wild ancestors and will be 100% outcrossing. They will be able to solve for themselves problems which are currently

Promiscuous tomato flower

being dealt with via poisons, materials, techniques, or labor. It may greatly simplify tomato growing in humid areas. The infusion of wild genetics added many delightful flavor profiles.

For years, this project has captured my attention, hopes, and dreams. I really want people in damp climates to be able to grow tomatoes organically, without sprays or unnecessary labor.

Genetic Bottlenecks

Domesticating tomatoes created a number of genetic bottlenecks. A bottleneck occurs when a small sample of a variety separates from the larger population. The small sample has a limited subset of genes. The limited genetic background creates inbreeding depression and loss of vigor. The new population may be missing genetic intelligence for dealing with specific pests, diseases, or environmental conditions.

The primary tomato bottlenecks included:

- Traveling from the Andes to Mexico.
- Traveling from Mexico to Europe.
- Traveling from Europe to the rest of the world.
- Decades of heirloom preservation inbreeding.

Tomato's accustomed pollinators didn't make the bottle-necking journeys with them. To cope, tomatoes became self-pollinating and highly inbreeding.

People selected against cross-pollination, inbreeding the heirlooms for fifty to hundreds of generations. Together, these events caused a loss of 95% of genetic diversity. Tomatoes today are among the most genetically-inbred and fragile crops. They are very susceptible to system-wide collapse.

Bottle-necking of tomato genetics

One study found more genetic diversity in a single wild tomato variety than in all the studied domestic lines combined.

The vast majority of tomatoes that I trial fail to ripen fruit. Breeding domestic tomatoes is problematic, because there is little diversity with which to work. There are a few colors and shapes of fruits, and a few leaf types. Overall, the domestic genome is severely limited in its genetic ability to deal with pests, diseases, and environmental stress. Domestic tomatoes have become imbeciles, forgetting the specie's ancestral intelligence.

Promiscuous Pollination

While conducting frost- and cold-tolerance trials, I noticed that the variety Jagodka frequently had bumblebees on the flowers. The rest of the patch rarely attracted pollinators. That got me thinking about selecting for more promiscuous tomatoes. A natural cross-pollination rate higher than the typical 3-5% would allow for quicker local adaptation.

During searches for promiscuous tomato flowers, we discovered the wild species Solanum pennellii and Solanum habrochaites. They require pollination by an unrelated plant. They are 100% outcrossing. Because they are incapable of pollinating themselves, they are called self-incompatible. They can only cross with a plant to which they are not closely related. The flowers are huge, colorful, and bold. Pollinators love them!

The wild species can donate pollen to domestic tomatoes. The cross doesn't work in the other direction.

S. pennellii and S. habrochaites are the two self-incompatible species that cross readily into domestic tomatoes. The other self-incompatible species rarely hybridize successfully with domestic tomatoes.

We made manual crosses between domestic tomatoes and the wild species of tomatoes, then re-selected for wild-type promiscuous flowers. The flowers are huge! The stigma (female part) is outside the anthers (male parts), so that they can rub against the belly of a bee. The primary selection criteria is for promiscuous flowers.

Exposed stigma

The most startling observation in this project was the tremendous diversity of aromas, tastes, and textures of the fruits. Descriptions by taste testers include words like: "melon," "yum," "xxx," "tropical," "fruity," "guava," "fermenty." We select for sweet, fruity, tropical flavors. We are selecting primarily for orange and yellow fruits, because of more favorable reviews.

Chef Barney Northrup said that he really wants me to replant seeds from the fruit that tasted like sea urchin. Whatever that is!

The offspring of the interspecies hybrids show tremendous diversity in many traits. I get reports of monster plants. I tend to select for dwarf determinate plants because they are super quick and highly productive. The dwarf determinate trait came from a domestic ancestor.

The traits for promiscuity are inherited, and selection for huge, colorful, open flowers is straightforward. Bumblebees and other species provide pollination services, so huge amounts of hybrid seeds can be generated without employing human labor. Three species hybrids are common.

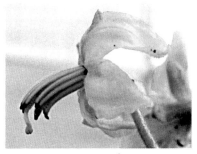

Open anthers

For a few years, we tried to re-select for a fully-functioning self-incompatibility system by observing lack of fruit set early in the season, or by culling any plants that set fruit when manually self-pollinated. Those are worthy goals, and someone that is very meticulous could advance the project a lot by doing that sort of work. We found it too cumbersome to do with thousands of plants and hundreds of collaborators. We are currently selecting for large, bright, open flowers.

The genes are known that control the self-incompatibility system. One day we might select by DNA testing.

It is an ongoing effort to train ourselves and collaborators to treat tomatoes as a promiscuous species. The traditional way to make tomato hybrids is one pollen donor to one mother. Then the offspring self-pollinate.

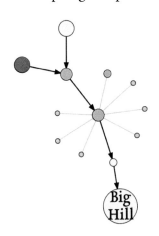

Pedigree of inbreeding tomato

It's been a challenge to get people to use a many-to-many approach. An early error in the project was not including enough wild pollen donors for the initial crosses. I recommend using 7 to 20 pollen donors for the initial crosses.

Compare the 1:1 pedigree for breeding a domestic tomato, which is shown on this page, with the many to many pedigree at the start of this chapter.

Introducing wild genetics decreased local adaptability in early generations. The offspring were often too long season for my garden. They weren't well adapted to the soil or climate. The plants that survived and thrived show hybrid vigor.

An early choice that caused ongoing fertility problems was making three-species hybrids (lycopersicum, habrochaites, pennellii). For those wanting to recreate this project from the beginning, I recommend choosing either S. pennellii or S. habrochaites as the pollen donor, but not both.

Wonderful fruity flavors are showing up along with acidic, funky tastes. We select each year for the flavors and aromas that please us. Because they are promiscuously pollinating, the odd flavors continue into future years, diminishing each year because we taste every fruit before saving seeds from them.

Auto-Generating Hybrids

A key component of permaculture is to let natural systems do most of the work. The steward only has to provide guidance from time to time.

The wild tomatoes have a self-incompatibility gene, which means that they cannot pollinate themselves. That makes them mandatory outcrossers. Every seed is a unique hybrid. Incorporating the gene into domestic tomatoes permits hundreds of thousands of unique genetic combinations to be easily, and automatically, created by the tomatoes themselves, eliminating the arduous labor that typically accompanies the creation of domestic tomato hybrids.

The multitudes of new genetic combinations can be trialed for dealing with bugs, viruses, blights, frost, weeds, flavor, color, etc. Self-incompatible tomatoes are self-breeding. They can solve for themselves problems that we have previously been trying to solve with sprays, chemicals, techniques, or labor.

We are seven to nine generations into incorporating the self-incompatible gene into domestic tomatoes.

We are also doing this project in the opposite direction, incorporating genes for larger fruits into wild tomatoes. This approach is called back-crossing.

Another aspect of this project is that we created locally-adapted populations of the purely wild species. We are domesticating them by selecting for larger, tastier fruits, and quicker maturity.

If I were to restart this project, I would use locally adapted, larger-fruited, tastier strains of the wild species as pollen donors.

Flower Types

The goal of this project is outcrossing tomatoes. One strategy for promiscuity is to incorporate the self-incompatibility system which makes them 100% outcrossing. We are working diligently on that aspect of the project. I use the term "promiscuous" to describe tomatoes that cannot pollinate themselves.

The other strategy is to select for flowers that facilitate outcrossing, even if the plant is also capable of self-pollinating. This strategy might make crossing as much as 10 times more likely than among domestic heirlooms. I use the term "panamorous" to describe tomatoes that are capable of self pollination, and that have flower traits that make crossing likely.

Tomatoes that outcross somewhat frequently are more resilient than tomatoes that rarely cross. Anything that can be done to encourage more crossing, in pure domestic tomatoes, is worthwhile.

Domestic flower
Anthers closed
Pollen trapped
Stigma hidden
Small/pale petals

Promiscuous flower
Anthers open
Pollen free-flowing
Stigma fully exposed
Large/colorful petals

Comparing inbreeding to promiscuous tomato flowers

The flowers on the promiscuous wild tomatoes are huge. Larger flowers are more attractive to pollinators. Wild flowers have bright colors. Domestic tomatoes have small, dull-colored flowers. Even on fully domestic tomatoes, outcrossing could be enhanced by selecting for larger, brighter petals. Outcrossing could be encouraged by close planting, alternating different varieties, and planting them crowded together, to increase naturally-occurring crosses. We could choose to favor crossing instead of self-pollination.

In domestic tomatoes, the anthers typically form a cone that completely encloses the stigma. This prevents pollen from entering, and from leaving, the flower. That trait, as much as any other, is responsible for the high selfing rates of domestic tomatoes. Loosely-connected anther cones are common in the promiscuous tomatoes. They may not even be connected at all. Domestic beefsteak tomatoes often have anther cones that are not tightly connected, thus contributing to their reputation of crossing more than other domestic tomatoes.

Anthers not connected

The promiscuous wild tomatoes often have long styles that extend the stigma beyond the anthers. This helps to facilitate crossing. Some of the domestic cherry tomatoes have retained this trait.

Some domestic tomatoes have petal arrangements that prevent bees from approaching the flowers. That's great for promoting self-pollination. It is counterproductive to biodiversity.

Sometimes, when I jostle the wild tomato flowers, a huge cloud of pollen falls out. That is a great trait for promoting cross-pollination, and attracting pollinators.

Tomatoes do not have nectaries. Therefore, honeybees have little interest in the flowers. Bumblebees and other native insects are the primary pollinators at my place. Ground-nesting digger bees are particularly active pollinating the tomato flowers.

Promiscuous, self-incompatible tomatoes require insects to pollinate them. At a minimum, I believe this means

Huge promiscuous flower vs. tiny inbreeding flower

not poisoning the insect population. A best practice is to plant pollinator-friendly plants nearby, and provide suitable nesting sites for ground-nesting bees and other pollinators.

Collaboration

The Beautifully Promiscuous and Tasty Tomato Project has attracted many collaborators. People obtained wild species from gene banks to share with me. Travelers come from across the continent to visit the plants. I mail fruits overnight to collaborators. We have taste testing get-togethers. We grew overwinter in greenhouses, in a warmer climate, to get extra generations. I traveled to farms and seed banks that are participating in the project.

Row 7 Seed Company facilitated winter crossing at Nipomo Native Seeds in California. William Schlegel and Andrew Barney made significant contributions, over many years. Andrea Clapp, at World Tomato Society, helps me develop strategies on how to proceed. Evan Sofro and John Cassia, at Snake River Earth Arts, grew a large field of the promiscuous tomatoes.

One area of particular interest, for this project, is growing these tomatoes, organically, without crop protection protocols or sprays, in areas where late blight is a problem. I'd love more collaboration on this project. Experimental Farm Network distributes the seed I grow for this project.

We are expecting that the rapid reshuffling of genetics in the Beautifully Promiscuous and Tasty Tomatoes will allow them to solve the late blight problem.

I think of the Beautifully Tasty and Promiscuous Tomato Project as my life's work. No matter how many other projects fall away due to limitations of strength, or ambition, the promiscuous tomato project continues. It is beautiful, tasty, and has the allure of chasing a pot of gold at the end of a rainbow.

Promiscuous vs. inbreeding
flower size comparison
(Actual size in the 6" x 9"
printed edition)

13 Corn

I love growing corn. It is robust, highly productive, and super easy to process. Corn is high in carbohydrates and energy. The various types of corn provide different culinary delights.

For me, corn produces the most calories for the least labor. The entire harvest process can be done with the human body alone. No tools or equipment are needed. Poultry can eat whole corn kernels.

Corn is less likely to produce the types of metabolic disorders that people experience when eating wheat.

For these reasons, if I were choosing one species to use as the primary staple crop for my village, it would be corn.

A disadvantage of corn in my ecosystem is that it requires irrigation. I grow small grains without irrigation by planting them in the fall. I can't do that with corn. Some ecosystems are able to support non-irrigated corn. Planting clumps far apart may reduce irrigation needs.

Corn has an outcrossing breeding system which makes it ideal for a landrace breeding project. It has a reputation of being susceptible to inbreeding depression. I adhere to the traditional wisdom that at least 200 plants should be planted for maintaining a corn variety.

In my ecosystem, most corn pollen falls approximately straight down most of the time. Most kernels are self-pollinated, or pollinated by the nearest neighbors.

The breeding method that I use with corn is recurrent mass selection. I plant the seed in bulk. I harvest seed from plants that thrive. An alternate method is sibling group selection, where a few seeds from each cob are planted. The whole sibling group is selected or culled as a unit.

A trait that I value in dry corn is easy shelling. I like the kernels to dislodge readily from the cob. The easy shelling trait is a high priority selection criteria. Sibling groups often share the easy shelling trait.

Sweet Corn

There are three types of sweet corn: old-fashioned, sugary-enhanced, and super-sweet. I focus on growing old-fashioned sweet corn as a landrace, because it is completely reliable for me.

The first landrace that I grew was an old-fashioned sweet corn.

Sugary-enhanced and super-sweet corn do not germinate reliably in cold spring soil. I grow sugary-enhanced sweet corn during the hottest time of year.

I do not grow super-sweet corn. The phenotype is also called shrunken. The seeds are shriveled. They lack enough resources to thrive. A related type of corn is called synergistic. It combines the three types of sweetness genes. It is likewise unreliable for me.

I love the taste of old-fashioned sweet corn. I love the chewy texture. When sweet corn is in season, I discard any dietary restrictions regarding carbohydrates. I love to eat old-fashioned sweet corn!

Sugary-enhanced sweet corn germinates better in early summer after the ground warms up. By then, it's flirting with not being ready before the fall frost.

As described earlier, I grow a sweet corn called Paradise. It is a hybrid that combines the wonderful flavor of old-fashioned sweet corn with the extra sweetness of sugary-enhanced sweet corn. Details about breeding that hybrid are in the chapter about making hybrids.

My favorite way to eat sweet corn is raw in the field. My next favorite way is boiled for 10 minutes. Sweet corn flavor deteriorates quickly. I like to pick it immediately before eating.

My tribe's harvest celebration includes throwing sweet corn onto the fire, still in its husks. They are buried in hot coals. We sing and dance for 15 minutes while they cook. Some parts come out charred. Some are almost raw. That's part of the charm of the harvest celebration.

Another way I enjoy eating sweet corn is parched in a hot fry pan, after removing dry kernels from the cob. I add a hint of oil to the pan. They puff up, but don't pop. Parched sweet corn is sweeter and more tender than parched flour corn. Parched sugary-enhanced sweet corn tastes especially delicious.

Popcorn

My popcorn originated as an accidental cross between a decorative flour corn and yellow popcorn. I loved the multi-colored cobs that showed up in the popcorn.

If I were to work on popcorn again, I wouldn't choose to make that particular cross. It took years to re-select for great popping. Each winter, I popped 20 kernels from each cob, using an electric frying pan set at 350° F. I replanted seeds from the cobs that popped best. I took both volume and percent popping into consideration. I tasted each cob. Non-delightful flavors and textures got culled.

I lost my popcorn project during a relationship meltdown. It was only lost to me, not to the community. Julie Sheen, at Giving Ground Seeds, sells it. Wayne Marshall, at Banbury Farm, grows Lofthouse Popcorn for Snake River Seed Cooperative.

Popcorn

I made crosses between high-carotene flint corn and landrace popcorn. The popped corn looks yellow. It looked wonderful, and tasted wonderful. I love the taste of carotenes in my food. Flint corn and popcorn are closely related. Therefore, selection for great popping is easier than with a cross to flour corn.

Flint Corn

Flint corn has hard, dense kernels. They look clear and glassy. I don't like flint corn in the kitchen, because it is hard on equipment. Flint corn flour has a gritty mouth feel. It sure is pretty. Wayne Marshall grows Glass Gem flint corn. He selects for great popping. Glass Gem contributed genetics to my popcorn landrace. I was growing it before its photo went viral.

Glass Gem flint corn

Grain Corn

Grain corn pleases me. It's the most genetically diverse corn that I grow. It adapts quickly to changing conditions. It combines many types of corn into one population without selecting by phenotype. Flint, dent, pop, sweet, and flour coexist.

Grain corn is great for brewing. My chickens love to eat it as whole-kernel feed. I use it as hominy.

In the 1960s plant breeders with Cargill adapted South American heritage corn races to grow in the long days of North

America. The seed sat in a freezer for decades. Joshua Gochenour acquired seed from five of the races and shared with me.

I made a hybrid swarm by crossing the five varieties together. I included Eagle Meets Condor, which is a north/south hybrid made by Dave Christensen. The next year, I crossed them to a hybrid swarm of heritage varieties from North America, which was put together by Andrew Barney. The South American corns are called flint, flour, and dent. The phenotypes are slightly different than phenotypes called by the same names in North American corns. The resulting hybrid swarm is highly diverse.

This corn, I call Harmony, because it combines the different diasporas of corn into a single breeding population. From this population, I selected the rest of the varieties described in this chapter.

An unexpected trait emerged among the descendants of Harmony. They were grown in a field frequented by skunks and raccoons, who feed heavily on corn. They underwent survival of the fittest selection. Each year, the corn got stronger and the animals took less. These days, predation is minimal.

High Carotene Flint

Cateto, one of the South American races, expresses up to ten times more beta-carotene than typical. I love the taste of carotenes in my food. It captivates me.

I selected a high carotene flint corn out of Harmony grain corn. Chefs love the high carotene trait, because of the taste and visual appeal. A deep orange cornbread looks great!

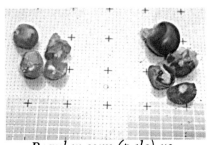
Regular corn (pale) vs. high carotene (dark)

When high carotene corn is fed to chickens, the carotenes concentrate into their eggs. The yolks become super colorful, and super tasty! Carotenes get stored in fat. High carotene chicken fat tastes wonderful, and looks amazing in a soup.

Flint corns are the most resistant to predation by insects, or larger animals. The hard kernels that make it more challenging to use in the kitchen also make it less desirable to predators.

High Carotene Sweet Corn

I crossed Astronomy Domine with the high carotene flint corn. The sweet trait is recessive, meaning that it doesn't show up in the first generation. Offspring resemble their parents and grandparents, and sometimes a trait skips a generation.

Sweet kernels showed up in the second generation. They were about ¼ of the kernels. The ¼ ratio is archetypal for describing the genetics taught in high school biology classes. The idea isn't often useful to me as a landrace plant breeder. There are usually so many genes involved in promiscuously pollinating crops that the math gets too complex. In the case of this sweet corn, there is only one gene difference between sweet corn and grain corn.

I selected for sweet corn, and the high carotene trait. I selected against all other colors. I tasted every cob before saving seeds from it by cutting off the end of the cob with hand shears. I culled any that were too fibrous, or lacked fabulousness.

Each year, I only save seeds from cobs that taste amazing. As a small scale grower, I can taste every plant, in every generation.

Andean Sweet

Harmony Grain corn contains a small amount of sweet corn genetics. I selected the wrinkled kernels from the cobs, and replanted them in isolation.

Andean Sweet was selected after Harmony had become resistant to skunks, raccoons, pheasants, and turkeys. Therefore, the plants are huge and strong. The cobs are high on the stalk.

Wrinkled sweet kernel on flour corn

The taste isn't my favorite. Any corn that is critter resistant and gets to the table is welcomed. Now that the sweet trait is stable, I can focus on selecting for taste.

The sweet trait is recessive. That means it can be hidden by other genes. Once a recessive trait is selected, it remains stable. In the photo that shows one sweet kernel on a cob of flour corn, at least half of the kernels have a hidden gene for sweetness. The sweet kernel shows up only because both the mother and the father each contributed one gene for sweetness.

Flour Corn

Flour corn carries the reputation of being the corn to grow for food security. My flour corn was selected from the predation-resistant strain of Harmony grain corn. I select for soft kernels, and against flinty types.

The local chefs love to cook with flour corn. They make bread, tortillas, posole, hominy, chicos, mush, and parched corn.

Flour corn kernels are soft, and easy to grind into flour. The flour is fine and light.

Flour corn makes tender hominy after nixtamalization. Tortillas or tamales made from nixtamalized flour corn are delicious! The taste of nixtamalized corn is another of those subtle nondescript flavors for which my body releases feel-good-chemicals. The non-nixtamalized corn typically sold in corn chips and tortillas seems ghastly to me.

Nixtamalization is cooking corn with a base. I prefer to use pickling lime. Traditionally, wood ashes were used. Cooking in a base dissolves or loosens the kernel's skin. I rinse the residues off using a colander. There are lots of recipes. Seems like everyone has their best practice. I use about two tablespoons of pickling lime to a gallon of corn. Cover with water, and boil till the skin loosens. That might take 20 to 60 minutes, depending on the variety of corn, and the type of base. Some recipes call for letting it soak overnight, either before or after cooking. I can't tell that it makes a difference.

I love the taste of nixtamalized corn so much that I won't buy tortillas or corn chips unless "lime" is listed as an ingredient.

I love to nixtamalize corn, and then dehydrate it. Followed by grinding to make masa harina. Nixtamalization converts the proteins into a form that is suitable for making dough. Plain ground corn only makes a gloppy paste.

Nixtamalization is critical for reducing mold toxins and for making niacin available, which protects against pellagra, a nutritional deficiency disease.

Air-rooted

A few years ago, scientists noticed nitrogen-fixing microbes living on corn's air-roots. The roots produce a gel containing food for the microbes. The microbes produce nitrogen for the corn. It is a classic symbiotic relationship.

The roots fell out of favor decades ago, because they form a knot that doesn't break down readily. It makes tilling and planting harder the next season. Modern industrialized agriculture selected against the air-root trait.

Upon hearing about the research, I selected a population that contains the air-root trait. Selection was

Corn air roots

primarily from Harmony, Lofthouse Flour, and High Carotene Flint. They are the populations in which the trait is most prevalent.

During damp weather, the air roots produce a gel. It tastes slightly sweet. I can't see microbes. I presume that they are living in the gel. The air-rooted stalks are among the tallest in my fields —like they were getting an extra dose of nitrogen. I don't fertilize or manure my fields. The crop residues and weeds from this year are next year's soil fertility. A corn that produces its own nitrogen has a competitive advantage.

14 Legumes

Legumes are a great source of plant based protein. As dry beans, productivity is low and labor high compared to other crops, but they provide protein that is not as readily available from other vegetables. Legumes may also be eaten as vegetables or greens.

The legumes occupy a wide range of ecosystems. For the sake of minimizing risk, I grow as many species as I can. A particular pest, disease, or weather pattern is unlikely to take them all out in the same growing season. Growing many species enhances food security.

Runner x common bean

Scarlet runner bean

Pea, lentil, fava, lupini, and garbanzo grow best in cool weather, and are frost resistant, perhaps even winter hardy. Common bean, tepary, cowpea, lima, and soybean grow best in hot weather. Some varieties of common bean and tepary are frost tolerant. Runner bean grows best in coastal areas with a maritime ecosystem. They are perennial in some areas.

Crossing Potential

The legumes typically self-pollinate, with outcrossing rates between 1% and 30%, depending on species and ecosystem. Gardens with healthier ecosystems, with more diversity of plants and insects, favor higher cross-pollination rates. Legumes cross at higher rates when closely inter-planted.

An easy way to notice naturally occurring hybrids in common beans, is to plant bush beans next to pole beans. In later years, if the bush bean offspring produce vines, then they are hybrids with the pole beans. One-fourth of the second generation will revert to being bush beans.

A bean with white flowers can be planted next to a bean with colored flowers. The next generation, if colored flowers show up in the white-flowered patch, then they are naturally-occurring hybrids. Andy Breuninger in Washington gave me an interspecies hybrid that he made by manually crossing common beans (as the mother) and scarlet runner beans as the pollen donor. The offspring had scarlet flowers. The color was faded compared to pure scarlet runner beans.

When sprouting, common beans send their cotyledons high into the air. Runner beans keep their cotyledons underground. The cotyledons of the hybrids stayed at or below ground level. That trait could be used to screen for hybrids.

When a row of common beans grows next to a row of runner beans, occasional cross-pollination occurs. The observant gardener can notice the naturally occurring hybrids, and plant them in higher numbers.

I receive naturally cross-pollinated beans from a number of friends and collaborators. Dave in Oregon grows beans as separate pure varieties. They grow in beds separated by a few feet. Perhaps 1 in 100 of the seeds that he harvests are a different color than expected. Those are natural hybrids. His wife only likes to cook pure varieties. She sorts them, removing the crossed beans before cooking. He gave me a pint jar of the crossed beans. I loved growing them. Lots of diversity among the offspring.

Tim Springston in New York noticed a naturally-occurring cross in his cornfield beans. He shared seed with me. One-fourth of the offspring were bush beans. I replanted the bush beans. I ate the pole beans. I found a delightfully colored bean that I've kept separate. Because common beans are highly inbreeding, it was easy to separate it from the landrace and maintain it as a pure cultivar.

Tim Morrison from my village saves his naturally occurring hybrids for me. I plant them and select for the types that I like. I really like the constant churning of the genetic lottery. The more often I plant mixed-up seed, the more likely I'll find something that really thrives here.

Fava Beans

Fava beans are a joy to work with. Their cross-pollination rate is around 30%. Bumblebees spend a lot of time with the fava beans. The natural outcrossing maintains diversity.

The first time I planted fava beans, I knew nothing about them. Since they are "beans," I planted them with the rest of the beans in the hottest time of the year. They flowered like crazy. The ants took up aphid farming on their leaves. They didn't make seeds. I read about them. The flowers are infertile when temperatures are high.

These days, I plant favas in early spring. I like to direct seed the day the

Fava beans

ground thaws. That is about the third week of March. The sooner they get going in early spring, the more they can flower in cool weather, and the more seeds they make. I often soak them overnight, before planting, for quicker germination.

Fava plants are winter hardy to zone 8. I recommend that people in warmer areas plant them in the fall. They are hardy down to about 10 °F (-12°C).

I experiment each year with growing favas as a fall planted crop. Timing matters. I have best results with seeds that go into the ground a day or two before the winter snow-cover arrives (early November). Young plants winter-kill. Seeds survive underground and get started a few weeks earlier than spring-planted seeds.

Each fall, my garden has a large population of volunteer fava plants going into winter. Many of them die in the fall. Some survive until spring, and then succumb. I keep watching them. Eventually one of them may survive a winter that is three zones colder than their preferred ecosystem.

That is the essence of landrace plant breeding: Pushing the limits, then watching for interesting things that survive and thrive.

Common Beans

Common beans cross at a rate of about 0.5 to 5%. I encourage crossing by closely inter-planting varieties. I watch for naturally-occurring hybrids, and plant them preferentially over the inbreeding varieties.

Each fall, I sort the common beans. I pick out about equal numbers of each type for replanting the next season. If I didn't plant in equal numbers, the little pink bean and the pinto beans would come to predominate in the population. They thrive here.

I select based only on phenotype of the seeds. If I make a pile of great white beans, they share the genes for big white seeds. Their genetics for other traits are variable.

I grow bean seed primarily for sharing and plant breeding. Therefore I want as much diversity as possible. If I were growing for food, I would plant primarily bulk seed. The most productive varieties would dominate.

Tepary Beans

People talk to me like I'm naughty for planting tepary beans. Supposedly they host a virus that devastates common beans. I wouldn't know. If a bean plant is susceptible to a virus, it dies. There are plenty of other families that are not susceptible.

I have grown tepary beans and common beans together for a decade. If there is a virus issue, they worked it out a long time ago.

Cooking

Seeds in general, and beans in particular contain anti-nutrients. Traditional cooking methods call for prolonged soaking of legume seeds, followed by cooking at high temperatures. Soaking, rinsing, and cooking with high heat reduce anti-nutrients.

I can taste the poisons in bean seeds. They taste medicinal to me. Something that I definitely don't want to be eating. I can taste the poison in green bean pods. The amount is much lower. Nevertheless, green beans are a food that I cook till well done. I prefer pressure cooking, or frying in hot oil instead of boiling. I wonder if the stomach upsets that are so common after eating beans are due to not deactivating the poisons?

The pods of tepary and lima beans taste particularly nasty. I stay away from them as a food source. Our primate bodies are very good about knowing when a plant is unsuitable as food.

Because traditional cooking methods reduce the poisons, I haven't been selecting against poisonous beans. I could pre-soak the seeds, to taste them before planting. Out of curiosity, I taste raw bean seeds. There is a lot of diversity in how poisonous they taste.

Sometimes, people feed me pancakes made from "garbanzo bean flour". The flour is made by milling raw garbanzo beans. The taste of poison is overwhelming. The traditional cooking method is to soak the beans. Pressure cook them. Mash them. Then deep fry to make falafel. Milling raw beans, and barely warming them in a pancake does not deactivate the poison.

I like pressure cooking bean seeds. The temperatures get hot enough to quickly and completely deactivate the poisons. Pressure cooking softens them much quicker in my high elevation kitchen.

Lupini beans are the most poisonous that I have tasted. The recipe for preparing them involves soaking for two weeks. Changing the water three times per day. An alternate method is to place them in running water for a week.

Slow cookers may not get hot enough to deactivate bean poisons. I recommend that they not be used for cooking beans. They work great for warming beans that have been thoroughly cooked by other methods.

Here is the recipe that I apply to cooking peas and beans.

- Rinse and sort. (No sense cooking pebbles.)
- Soak in cold water for 8 to 36 hours, change the water and rinse every 4 to 8 hours. I typically start beans soaking in the morning, that I will cook the next day.
- Bring to a hard boil for 10 minutes. Turn off heat. Soak for one hour. Rinse.
- Combine with other ingredients and cook until soft.

15 Squash Family

Squash, melons, cucumbers, and gourds are naturally outcrossing. They have male flowers and female flowers on the same plant. Bees move pollen between flowers. Due to their high rate of promiscuity, species from the squash family are an excellent choice for starting to explore landrace gardening and seed saving.

Watermelon

I select for yellow-fleshed watermelons, because the chemical that causes red coloration in melons (and tomatoes) is bitter. I can grow melons with lower sugar content, that taste sweeter, because they don't need extra sweetness to overcome the bitterness.

Yellow watermelon

Pepo

Pepo squash include crookneck, zucchini, acorn, Delicata, jack-o-lantern, and decorative gourds. They are the quickest maturing winter squash. They are often eaten as summer squash.

The decorative gourds are closely related to a wild ancestor, and may contain bad tasting poisons. I discourage using decorative gourds in plant breeding, unless you want to put in the effort of tasting to eliminate the poisons.

For many years, I avoided growing pepo winter squash. I thought they were gaggy. Many pepo squash have pale white flesh. I love carotenes in my food. Pepo squash are low in carotenes.

Due to customer requests, I started growing pepo winter

Acorn/Delicata grex

squash. I followed my usual protocol of tasting every squash in every generation before saving seeds. These days, I don't whine about tasting the pepo winter squash. You get what you select for. I select for flavor and more colorful flesh.

I grow a hybrid swarm of Delicata and acorn squash. If I cared about preserving the shapes, I could plant them as sister lines, with Delicata on one end of the row, and acorn on the other. My primary selection criteria is for taste and colored flesh. I don't care about the shape, or color of the skin.

I grow yellow crookneck. I keep it stable for crooked neck, and yellow skin. Other traits vary.

Landrace marrows

I grow zucchini. I keep them stable for long, skinny fruits. Skin color can be dark green, light green, yellow, beige, white, or striped. I select for bushy plants. Mature zucchini that are being grown for seed make decent winter squash, called marrows. I select the marrows for taste, and easy cutting.

Moschata

The butternut family of squash has a reputation of being the most resistant to pests and diseases. The vine and peduncle are hard, making them resistant to vine borers. The flavor is better than pepo, but not as good as maxima. They retain high quality during long storage.

Lofthouse landrace moschata squash

The year I started a moschata landrace, the growing season was 88 days long, and 75% of the varieties failed to make fruits. I harvested immature fruits, which matured indoors for a few months before harvesting seeds. In the third year, they produced abundant mature fruit in an 84-day growing season.

I planted butternut-shaped squash, long-necked squash, and round pumpkins. They cross-pollinated. The offspring were many shapes and sizes. Customers at farmer's market were leery. Many had never seen a round butternut before.

I've mentioned that landraces belong to a community. This was my first introduction to that idea. My customers learned that anything I take to market tastes fantastic. Doesn't matter what shape, color, or size of fruit. My customers took a strong liking to the long-necked shape. Therefore, I preferentially plant seeds for the long-necked phenotype. I grow about 90% long-necked, and 10% pumpkins. That keeps the long-necked phenotype dominant, while maintaining genetic diversity.

People that buy seed from me ask for smaller fruits. I started saving seeds from the smallest fruits each year. I grew them in a separate field. Eventually, the fruits were much smaller than half a pound. I didn't like them. They didn't store well. The seeds were small, lacking energy to grow quickly. The small plants lacked vigor. I didn't share the seed from them. A variety has to please the farmer before it can become beloved by a community. As a subsistence farmer, larger fruits provide more food for the same labor and space. I aim to produce varieties with fruits weighing between 5 to 15 pounds.

Maxima

I love maxima squash. They grow vigorously. They taste savory and sweet. They mature quickly. Productivity is wonderful. They produce an abundance of carotenes. Storage lifetime averages three to five months.

Maxima squash produce thick succulent stems, and corky peduncles. Vine borers ravage them in many places. People don't even try to grow them. They don't like fighting the vine borers.

What if we could combine the wonderful taste of maxima with the vine-borer resistance of moschata?

The common squash species don't normally cross with each other. I found one naturally-occurring hybrid in 12 years. I grow thousands of squash per year.

An inter-species hybrid, named Tetsukabuto, exists. It is a cross between maxima and moschata. Astute plant breeders in Japan created it. Pinetree Garden Seeds sells seeds. The male flowers shrivel up before producing pollen. I grew Tetsukabuto in my squash patch. The other squash provided pollen. Bees distributed pollen.

I replanted the seeds. The first year, I selected for restored fertility. In later years, I selected for savory maxima flavor, and skinny, hard vines. Grow reports from infested areas say that the squash are resistant to vine borers. I'm calling this population Maximoss. I'd love for others to repeat this process.

I selected in the other direction also, for fruits with the butternut shape. I call this population Moschamax. Some of the offspring picked up the orange skin of the maxima buttercups. I haven't yet found a version that incorporates the savory maxima flavor, and the butternut shape. The selection process would go easier if I were willing to do manual pollination between selected parents.

Flavor

Before I save seeds from any squash fruit, I taste it. I taste around 16 fruits at a time. I taste them raw, and cooked.

Selecting the best-tasting squash

While taste testing, I pay attention to how well the fruit stored. I notice how easily it cuts or peels. I smell each fruit. I examine the color. If anything seems off about the fruit, I feed it to the chickens. I only save seeds from fruits that are pleasing in every way.

I love the taste of carotenes in my food. The more carotenes, the better tasting. This trait is particularly noticeable in squash. Year by year, my squash become darker orange. I love them a little more each year.

Cooking

I love eating cooked squash. Any species of squash can be eaten as summer squash, while immature and tender. My favorite is crookneck, because it is high in the carotenes that I love. Saute in a hot pan, with oil. Fry until brown. Season with salt and pepper. I don't like boiling or steaming summer squash, because they get mushy, and that gags me. My mother adds grated summer squash to cakes and cookies. We freeze grated squash for that use during the winter.

Tasting many fruits

I cook winter squash in a similar manner. Cut into half-inch (1 cm) thick slices. Fry in oil until soft. Long-necked butternuts are fun to cook this way, because they form round disks. I selected the long-necked butternuts to have tender skin. That allows easy peeling with a potato peeler, or eating soft delicate skins.

We bake winter squash in the oven at 350° F (180° C) for about an hour, or until tender. We bake them as half-fruits or cut into fries. If baked as fries, we toss them with oil prior to cooking.

Sliced long-necked squash

Any leftovers get mashed and frozen to be used as pumpkin pie filling. I also make pumpkin pie filling by pressure canning squash in quart jars. Home-bottled squash is golden colored and light tasting, far different from the brown glop that the machines produce.

I cook with singing, dancing, joyfulness, and gratitude. I think that it makes a difference in how the food tastes. It certainly makes a difference in my attitude towards food. I take better care of myself when I know that the food I eat has been blessed by my care and attention.

16 Grains

Growing and storing small grains enabled civilization. They are easy to grow and harvest with simple tools and methods. Their huge productivity, high calories, and long storage allowed for centralization of the food supply. People could be co-opted for other activities like literacy, art, science, music, mining, construction, manufacturing, commerce, and politics.

The high productivity of grains continues into the present day, and can act as a source of freedom from centralization. Grains are POWERFUL for good or evil.

For an hour of moderately hard labor, I can harvest enough grain to feed myself for a week. Looking at it the other way, a year's worth of grain only costs me one week of labor to harvest. Planting and tending the growing plants might take up another week. The grains are low in vitamins. They don't provide balanced nutrition.

Growing

I subsistence farm, growing organically in a low-input system. That influences what types of grains I value. I want grain to be about waist high. I don't want to stoop over to harvest. Taller grains outgrow the weeds, which saves weeding labor. People say that taller grains are more susceptible to lodging. I don't harvest seeds from lodged plants, thus selecting for anti-lodging.

I haven't applied poisons, herbicides, fertilizers, composts, nor manures to my current field since I started growing in it 12 seasons ago. I select for plants that thrive in spite of the soil, climate, diseases, pests, and predators. When they get to a field that is manured, they really thrive. I don't want my farming systems to depend on far away mega-entities.

In my ecosystem, Cache Valley Rye naturalized. It grows on the side of the road, on the hills, and in other non-mowed places. It doesn't require irrigation. It establishes itself with the fall rains, and overwinters. It grows under the snow!

In the spring, it outgrows the weeds. In non-irrigated areas, it reaches 3-4 feet (1 m) tall. In irrigated fields, it grows to 6 feet (2 m). It works great as a no-till, self-reseeding crop. There are enough feral patches to feed anyone that wanted to harvest the seeds.

What a wonderful cropping system. The winter rains provide the moisture for the crop. It avoids weed pressure by growing when weeds lie dormant. I rake the plants a few times in the spring. Raking kills the delicate annual weed seedlings, without harming the grain.

Oats usually winter kill at my place. In some years, a few survive. In other years, they all die. Oats are not reliably hull-less for me. That makes them unpleasant to eat. I focus, for now, on easy hulling. If that gets resolved, then I may try selecting for winter hardiness.

Many varieties of wheat reliably over-winter for me. My great-great grandfather's wheat grew as a non-irrigated winter wheat.

When growing small amounts of grains, if they are spaced widely (1 foot apart, 0.3 m), they produce many tillers per plant (up to 350 seeds). For rapid seed-increase, I use wide spacing.

Harvesting

The tools that I use for harvesting and cleaning small grains are my body, gloves, shoes, bypass shears, a tarp, a stick, and buckets. Harvesting grains with substitutions or omissions of these items is very possible.

Easy threshing is important to me. I harvest with hand shears, and thresh with my feet, or by beating with a stick. Because I harvest by hand, I don't need uniform maturity dates.

I select heavily for non-shattering, allowing the grain to stand in the field for a long time. I select for early maturity as a primary selection criteria. Longer maturing grains are more at risk to winds, rains, disease, and predators. I love genetic diversity, because one pest, or one disease, doesn't take out a whole field, it only takes out some plants.

The technique I use is to walk down the row, grabbing a handful of grain, and cutting it off with shears or a blade. I toss the seed heads onto a tarp. I jump up and down on them, or beat them with a stick. After they are thoroughly threshed, I pour them from bucket to bucket, in a wind, to separate the grain seeds from the chaff. This is called winnowing. A piece of coarse screen or a colander can be helpful for separating larger chaff from the small seeds prior to winnowing. The majority of the chaff can be raked off before winnowing.

When growing grains, I select for plants that grow about waist high, because then I can easily harvest them while standing up.

Some types of grains are readily harvested by grabbing the heads and yanking to separate the head from the stalk. I like to wear gloves and shoes, because the chaff can puncture skin.

Breeding

The Rocky Mountain Seed Alliance hosts the Heritage Grain Trials. We are collecting, growing, and scaling up historical grain varieties. Seedkeepers, gardeners, farmers, chefs, and bakers collaborate on the project. My early role in the project was scaling up a few pinches of seeds to a few cups. I successfully grew wheat, barley, rye, and oats. I was unsuccessful with millet. I didn't like the shattery oats, so I didn't volunteer to grow them a second time.

After a few years, my fields became weedy with grains. I couldn't grow pure varieties for the project any more. Therefore, we started projects to breed landrace wheat and barley. While I was trialing and increasing the quantities of seed, other gardeners were doing the same thing. Lee-Ann Hill, project manager, sent me about 16 varieties of each species, which are known to thrive in the Rocky Mountains. I added a few of my favorites, including my great-great grandfather's wheat.

Wheat and barley cross at about 10% in dry climates. Crossing is lower in damp climates. We jumbled the varieties together to encourage cross-pollination. Both populations thrived when spring planted.

Occidental Arts and Ecology also sent seeds, descended from about 2000 varieties of wheat. I planted them in the same field, on the same day. Occidental is on the California coast. The seeds were not adapted to growing in the desert, at high elevation, in the Rocky Mountains. The vast majority of the plants flowered at shin-height. I did not like that, because I don't like stooping to harvest. Some plants grew tall and vigorous. I saved seed from them, and combined them into a common seed lot with the Heritage Grain Trials varieties. The Occidental seed contributed about 15% to the total harvest. It was about 60% of the seeds that were planted.

The Occidental population was much more diverse than the Heritage Grain Trials population. Much of the diversity did not get preserved, because it didn't meet my needs as a farmer. I didn't harvest short plants, nor plants that matured in late fall. Some of the Occidental plants required a winter before flowering. They didn't flower.

I returned seed to the grain trials. I sent the wheat and barley grexes to Experimental Farm Network as "Rocky Mountain Wheat" and "Rocky Mountain Barley". I shared with bakers.

I loved the wheat. It grew robustly. The plants were tall and easy to harvest without stooping.

The barley plants were shorter. I only collected seeds from the tallest plants that didn't fall over from wind or irrigation. I want the population to move in the direction of being easier to harvest.

I replanted the seeds. Some hybrids showed up as indicated by new phenotypes appearing in the bulk, and by off-types appearing in sibling group plantings. I again collected seeds, and returned them to the grain trials, and shared with Experimental Farm Network.

Because wheat and barley are weedy in my garden, I inadvertently select for winter hardiness. It's likely that I'll end up growing sister-lines separated into a spring-planted population and a fall-planted population. I may seed the wildlands with the fall-planted populations, and allow them to fend for themselves. Wheat is not currently feral in my community. If enough diversity is planted, something might become feral.

I use the term "winter wheat" to indicate that I planted the seeds in the fall, and they survived the winter. I use the term "spring wheat" to indicate that I planted the seeds in the spring. Some grains require chilling before they flower. Planting in early spring can provide the necessary chill.

Some varieties might be exclusively winter wheat or exclusively spring wheat. Most of the varieties that I grow can be planted either way. I tend to think of barley as a spring-planted crop.

The genetics of wheat is complex. I jumbled all types together. They can work it out among themselves.

Some varieties are much more outcrossing than others. I noticed that the anthers on the more outcrossing varieties were outside the husk. Over time, growing grains landrace style will tend to select for higher outcrossing rates.

Perennial Grains

I grow small patches of perennial wheat and perennial rye. Folklore says that they originated as interspecies hybrids with wild grasses. The permaculture allure is that you can plant once and not disturb the soil again. My initial goal with these species was to select for winter hardiness. I'm currently selecting for ease of threshing. I received my original seed stock from Jason Padvorac. He wrote:

> Many hill peoples gather and tend perennial grains that grow wild. Anyone wanting to learn about perennial grains would do well to look into the grains that local indigenous people work with, and how they do that.
>
> Some perennial grains have a very short productive lifespan and in early commercial production are tilled in every two or three years. Another reason they do that is because the field begins to become a grassland ecosystem and the perennial grain stops being the primary plant, and they want a higher yield per acre. Some have a long lifespan, but can choke themselves out without some kind of management or disturbance. This makes a huge difference for management, and to what degree we really can just "plant once and not disturb the soil."
>
> If we want to grow perennial grains without regular disturbance, we have to mimic the ecology of grassland. Natural grasslands have a mixture of grasses and forbs that will find some natural balance. Making sure that the balance includes a high percentage of the grains we want to grow requires some combination of luck, local expertise, and skillful management. Without a good deal of luck, it will require a lot of expertise and skill.
>
> Over time, the original parents will die off, and new perennial grain children will need to become established. Unless one is lucky, careful observation of their habits of establishment is likely necessary in order to keep a high percentage of perennial grains in the field.
>
> On land that wants to grow into forest, at a minimum the field must be mowed, burned, or grazed yearly to keep down brambles and trees. On any land, the thatch must at a

minimum be knocked to the soil so that nutrients can cycle and so that the dry thatch doesn't choke out the new growth.

In the big picture, if we want to plant a crop that will just give us food for many many years, plant a tree. If we want to grow perennial grains without tilling them in every two years, what we are really growing is a grassland ecosystem. An ecosystem is not a crop, it is a sophisticated living entity. It is well worth tending food at the level of ecosystem, but we must be humble and understand our limitations, and not expect an ecosystem to act like a monoculture field.

In terms of breeding, if we are growing perennial grains in a natural ecosystem setting, they will be self seeding to meet *their* criteria for survival, not our criteria for productivity or ease of harvest. They will naturally become wilder and less domesticated, and generally look more and more wild. By managing the field to control the circumstances under which seedlings can get established (by flooding, mowing, periodic strip tilling, weeding, livestock grazing, trampling, or whatever) we can sow selected seed and continue to boost the genetics of our choice.

Cooking

Because of the anti-nutrients in grain, people's health and well-being suffered when societies switched from hunter/gatherer to grain-based agriculture. New diseases and ailments appeared among the civilized. The effects are noticeable today by observing the rampant obesity, malnutrition, and metabolic disorders common in civilizations and families that rely on grains. Traditional cooking methods (sourdough, whole grain, sprouting), minimize the anti-nutrients and increase vitamins. They take time and labor which the industrialized food system is not willing to spend.

Many people suffer from low-level allergies to recently developed grain varieties and harvesting techniques. These occur less frequently with grains and methods that were commonly used more than 60 years ago.

Best practices for reducing anti-nutrients include eating whole seeds that have been soaked, sprouted, and/or fermented before boiling, and discarding the cooking water. Traditional sourdough cooking is a slow process, to allow time for the breakdown of anti-nutrients.

I don't like to eat unidentifiable glops. I don't have a clue what the factory bakers add to breads, cakes, cookies, or puddings.

I believe that people's health would improve dramatically if we stopped eating unidentifiable food-like substances. I don't like eating foods unless I can tell by looking at them what species they are.

Decker five seed—Crumb Brothers Artisan Bread

17 Landrace Everything

The principles of food security through biodiversity, which are the focus of this book, apply to every part of the natural world. I believe that they should be applied to the animals that we keep on our homesteads and farms. In this chapter, I'll discuss chickens, honeybees, mushrooms, and trees.

It is easier to maintain high populations of plants than animals. Animals are more noticeably affected by inbreeding depression than plants, warranting extra care. To maintain high population sizes, landrace animal breeding is more easily done by communities than by individuals.

Another nuance with animal breeding is that I cull more, based on maladaptive traits, than with plants.

The inbreeding that it takes to maintain a breed results in predictable ailments.

I love mixed-breed farm animals, because of their extra resilience. Feral cats and mixed breed dogs make me happy.

Chickens

Heritage breeds of chickens tend to be highly inbred. People love their heritage breeds, and go to great lengths to make sure that the inbreeding continues. I've read reports of maintaining some breeds as a single breeding pair!

Heritage breed preservation is another example of a variety that was selected to thrive long ago, on a far away farm. Modern conditions and the local ecosystem in each coop are different from whatever they were when and where the breed originated.

Landrace chickens adapt more easily to local conditions: the weather, a particular coop, the farmer's and community's habits.

I know farmers who keep large flocks of mixed breed chickens, which are allowed to interbreed at will. Their flocks survive fine. I think that is partially because they keep large flocks, and they maintain large numbers of roosters in the flock.

The historical way of avoiding inbreeding depression in a flock is to keep only the hens hatched on your homestead, and then bring in unrelated roosters from elsewhere. Unrelated means separated by three or more generations.

Traditionally, this method coalesced into a method known as spiral breeding. It is named spiral because the male chicks move

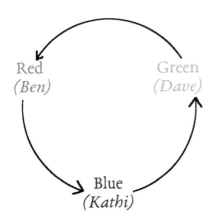

Red
(Ben)

Green
(Dave)

Blue
(Kathi)

Spiral Breeding:
Rooster chicks go to new flock

from flock to flock, preventing them from mating with close relatives.

Spiral breeding involves maintaining three or more flocks of chickens. No males remain in their mother's flock. Young roosters move to the next flock in the spiral. The order of rotation is always the same. For example Red Flock → Blue Flock. Blue Flock → Green Flock. Green Flock → Red Flock. That maintains an inbreeding distance of three generations.

Keep enough roosters in each generation so that if one dies unexpectedly, the spiral can continue. A rooster that stays with the flock for years has more influence over the genetics of the flock than younger roosters. Younger roosters contribute to quicker adaptation. Older roosters add stability.

For simplicity, spiral breeding is best done with three or more flocks of chickens on multiple homesteads. Ben gives his rooster chicks to Kathi. She gives hers to Dave. Dave gives his to Ben. Always in that order. Then no record keeping or pedigrees are required.

Spiral breeding can also be done on a single homestead, by putting colored bands on each bird when they are young. They can be kept as a mixed flock for most of the year, being separated only for the duration of mating season. I know a homesteader who does spiral breeding by memorizing which birds belong to which flock.

To preserve local adaptation while increasing genetic diversity, I recommend that one or two hens in ten be a new breed, imported from outside the spiral each year. Any random breeds are fine, as there's no telling who will contribute a gene that would be beneficial to the long-term viability of the flock.

If you really can't find neighbors who share your vision about landrace chickens, there is a variation on the spiral breeding theme. Keep only your hens. Each spring before mating season, get rid of all of your roosters, and bring in roosters from random breeds that haven't been on your farm before. That keeps the local adaptation of the hens, and is constantly bringing in new diversity from the roosters.

Culture is an important part of a chicken's survival ability. The best way for them to learn survival skills is from their mother, and the other members of the flock. I highly recommend that locally-adapted landrace chicken flocks self-sustain with broody hens, and not by robotic hatching machines.

Many modern and heritage breeds have lost the instinct for brooding. Developing a robustly thriving locally-adapted flock of chickens might involve selecting for broodiness.

Honeybees

About 70% of the honeybee colonies in the U.S. are trucked to the almond orchards in California each spring. The bees exchange pests and diseases with each other before migrating to the rest of the country. The ecosystem of the orchards is bare dirt. The ecosystem provides little benefit to the bees. By the next spring, 40% of the colonies have died.

In my valley, the current winter death rate of honeybees is nearly 100%, regardless of beekeeper preparations. In the spring, the bees get replaced by non-locally adapted bees that have just come back from California. Disease and pests are rampant. The bees are dependent on chemicals for survival. They lack local adaptation. They stand little chance of surviving the winter.

My great-grandfather and father were beekeepers, keeping locally-adapted honeybees without winter preparations, except for minimizing the entrance

Industrialized beekeeping

size. Feral honeybees lived in rock formations in the surrounding hills and in abandoned buildings. The local do-gooders took it upon themselves to kill the feral honeybees, claiming that they were a bio-hazard.

For the sake of local food security, my valley ought to bring back locally-adapted bees, both managed and feral. I'm going to present some ideas about what I think a best practices development project might look like.

The project should be treatment free. No chemical treatments. No antibiotics. No mite treatments. By running a treatment-free system, the pests, diseases, and honeybees can enter into stable relationships.

The bees should build natural honeycomb in random patterns. Commercially-available foundation has an unnatural cell size. When bees hatch from industrialized comb, they grow to an unsuitable size for their biology. Straight combs interfere with proper heating and cooling of the hive.

The concept of an apiary should be eliminated. To minimize drift of bees and diseases, place colonies at least 80 yards (73 m) apart, with entrances askew, and different geometric patterns painted on each colony.

Warré hives may be the most suitable for my climate, built with 1.5 to 3 inch (4 to 8 cm) or thicker wood for added temperature stability, and with a natural compost floor.

Natural swarming patterns, from small hives, should be the normal mode of reproduction.

If possible, do the project in an area that is not swamped by drones from California. Perhaps offer locally-adapted bees to people whose bees winter kill. That way, the recipients would be contributing project-adapted drones to the mating pool.

Like all natural systems, the bees will adapt to whatever they have to work with. The closer our designed system can match their natural state, the more easily they adapt. I highly recommend *12 Tenets Of Preservation Beekeeping* which is available from What Bees Want.

An education component would be required, in order to teach the local bee inspector and chemical beekeepers that locally-adapted bees are not a bio-hazard.

The project should periodically import genetically-dissimilar strains of bees, especially if they are from other projects that are working on developing treatment-free, locally-adapted, landrace populations.

A honeybee breeding project, more than any other that I have discussed in this book, is a whole-community project. Community outreach could be important to encourage people to value feral colonies and hold them in high esteem.

Mushrooms

The mating system of mushrooms seems mysterious. They respond well to landrace gardening. I collect mushrooms in the wild and from the store. I blend them into a watery purée. I dump the solution onto suitable habitats. Then after rainstorms during cool weather, I check on the plantings. Once established, a mushroom patch may fruit for many years.

The mushrooms I grow are outdoors in a living ecosystem. They thrive in the natural world.

Morel mushrooms grow in association with cottonwood, poplar, and aspen. If I plant them on wood chips, I prefer to use those tree species.

I most commonly find oyster mushrooms growing from tree roots. When I plant them intentionally, I mimic that ecosystem by partially burying the logs. It's very dry here. Burying the logs helps keep them moist.

Like any species, you get what you select for, and the species adapts to conditions as they are. The more diversity you have in the environment, the more local adaptation is possible.

Trees

Trees are a long-term breeding project, perhaps multi-generational. When breeding trees, I take a happy-go-lucky approach. Before the seedlings mature, the land is likely to have switched owners. Perhaps multiple times. I plant as many tree seedlings as possible. A decade or two later, when the trees are bearing seeds, I knock on the door of whomever is stewarding the land and ask for seeds.

I sell tree seedlings at farmer's market. I might not know where they go. Years later, I may find them growing around town.

I plant tree seeds and seedlings into the wildlands. Some of them get established.

The offspring of great parents tend to be great. I don't find new poisons or freaks when I grow trees from seed. Most typically the offspring closely resemble their parents.

Apples

My community dug irrigation ditches when it was established 160 years ago. The workers buried the seeds of their lunch apples near the canal. Apple trees still grow along the canal. The apples are mostly small-fruited, with yellow skins. Flavor is tart and bright. Every tree produces different tasting fruit. I haven't found any that are bitter or inedible. They are not bothered by codling moth worms. Feral apple trees grow in riparian areas throughout the valley.

Walnuts

My walnut breeding project is carrying on the work that was started by Les Shandrew. He passed away many decades ago. He grew two generations of trees. I heavily selected the third generation for winter hardiness. I moved the seedlings 900 feet (0.27 km) higher in elevation. The expanded range allows Carpathian walnuts to grow in a valley that is too cold for reliable production of commercially available clones.

The third generation has started producing nuts. One tree has sweet nutmeats, without the bitterness I dislike in walnuts. We are planting fourth-generation seedlings around town.

Apricots

Apricots grow feral in my ecosystem, without irrigation. When my daddy was a boy, he ate apricots on a dry hilltop. The pits stayed behind. Seventy years later, a seedling has become a grove. Apricot seedlings fruit in three to five years. A person can hope to grow a number of generations in a lifetime.

I grow a row of apricot seedlings. One of the parents is sweet and delicate. If picked, it has to go from hand to mouth, because it lacks shipping qualities. It is an amazingly old-fashioned flavor delight. I hope that some of its offspring will taste as good.

Landrace nuts

Landrace beets

Afterword

I presented my ideas about how landrace gardening strengthens local food and seed production. I shared that food security improved on my farm due to local adaptation, genetic diversity, and cross-pollination.

I touched briefly on how we got to where we are. My focus is not on being angry at bad guys. My intent is to build systems that we love in our own lives. The rest of the world can live in their chosen systems.

The first draft of this book contained a chapter entitled "Community." It was removed in favor of spreading the idea through the entire book. Landrace gardening is as much about thriving local communities as it is about plants.

I presented a way out of the stresses of keeping heirlooms pure and isolated. I noted that populations are stronger if they are cross-pollinating and genetically-diverse. I suggested minimizing or eliminating record keeping.

I gave examples of crops I have worked on. I commented that by paying attention, crops can diverge in new and exciting directions. Selection can create new varieties for new agricultural practices.

I shared my passion regarding the Beautifully Promiscuous and Tasty Tomato project. I hope some of you will join me in creating a robust population of self-incompatible tomatoes.

I noted species with potential for ongoing breeding work. I wrote about a few dozen species. I have worked on a hundred. There are thousands more in other ecosystems, and in the wildlands. The principles of landrace gardening apply to any ecosystem, and any plant or animal population. We get what we select for, even if it is inadvertent. Genetically-diverse, cross-pollinating populations adapt to changing conditions. This leads to a more reliable food security.

Beginning can be as easy as growing a few plants each, of two varieties close together, then saving seeds and replanting. What species do you feel inspired to adapt to landrace gardening?

Appendix

Ease of Developing Landrace Crops

This table summarizes my attitude towards the difficulty of creating landraces using various species[1]. Annual species that are highly outcrossing convert most quickly into locally-adapted landraces. Large flowers make it easy to create freelance hybrids.

Crop	Crossing Rate	Freelance Hybrids	Avoid F1 Hybrids[2]
Very Easy			
Bean, Fava	~30%	yes	
Bean, Runner	~35%	yes	
Corn	high	easy	
Cucumber	~70%	easy	
Melons	high	easy	
Spinach	100%	easy	
Squash	high	easy	
Easy			
Asparagus	100%	easy	
Barley	~10%		
Cabbage, Kale, Broccoli	100%	yes[3]	yes
Eggplant	~10%	yes	
Okra	~10%	yes	
Pepper	~10%	yes	
Radish	~85%		yes

1 For non-listed species, you can estimate the ease of conversion to landrace gardening by looking at the flowers. If they are annuals that attract lots of pollinators, or if they use wind dispersal of pollen, they are on the easier end of the scale.
2 Commercial hybrids are often made using cytoplasmic male sterility.
3 Because this species is self-incompatible, freelance hybrids are easy by planting exactly one plant of each variety to be crossed.

Crop	Crossing Rate	Freelance Hybrids	Avoid F1 Hybrids
Sunflower	~50%		yes
Tomatillo	100%	yes	
Tomato, Panamorous	~30%	yes	
Tomato, Promiscuous	100%	easy	
Wheat	~10%		
Hard [4]			
Beet	high		yes
Carrot	high		yes
Onion	high		yes
Parsnip	~30%		yes
Potato		yes	
Rutabaga	~20%		yes
Sweet Potato	100%		
Tomato, domestic [5]	~3%	yes	
Turnip	100%		yes
Very Hard [6]			
Bean, common	0.5-5%	yes	
Bean, garbanzo	low	yes	
Garlic			
Lettuce	~3%		yes
Pea	0.5%	yes	
Sunroot [7]	100%		

4 I classify biennial root crops as hard, due to the difficulty of overwintering roots.
5 I consider domestic tomatoes hard, because of limited genetic diversity.
6 I put species with low cross-pollination rates into the very hard category.
7 I call sunroots very hard, due to weediness.

Quick Summary

Landrace

- Locally-adapted
- Genetically-diverse
- Promiscuously-pollinating
- Community-oriented

Grand Secret of Plant breeding

- Plants make seeds
- Offspring resemble their parents and grandparents
- Sometimes a trait skips a generation.

Creating a Landrace

- Heirloom and open-pollinated varieties preferred
- Mass cross or incremental change
- Promiscuous pollination
- Survival of the fittest
- No coddling
- Use local varieties

Maintaining a Landrace

1. Community, Community, Community
2. Add new genetics
3. Keep older genetics
4. Prefer larger populations
5. Select liberally
6. Prioritize crossing

Seed Harvest

Dry
- Thresh
- Screen
- Winnow

Wet
- Ferment
- Rinse
- Dry
- Winnow

Seed Storage
- Cold
- Dark
- Dry
- Secure

Have Joy In The Garden
- Hugs
- Singing
- Dancing
- Storytelling
- Community
- Drum circles
- Walk barefooted
- Foraging hand to mouth
- Bonfires and full moon howls
- Parties for planting and harvest
- Savoring wonderful fresh flavors
- Hide pretty stones to find years later while weeding

Graphics Index

Alphabetical Index

About the Author

Joseph Lofthouse learned seed keeping from his grandfather and father, on a sixth-generation family farm.

He worked as a chemist before melting down due to the ethical dilemmas. He sought refuge in a monastery, taking a vow of poverty, before returning to farming in his home village.

He grew market vegetables for three years then transitioned to seed keeping, landrace development, speaking, and writing.

Experimental Farm Network is the near-exclusive distributor of seeds grown on Joseph's farm. Giving Ground Seeds sells many varieties. Snake River Seed Cooperative distributes some varieties grown by regional farmers. Baker Creek Heirloom Seeds sells Astronomy Domine sweet corn. The following seed companies carry a few varieties: Wild Mountain Seeds, Seed Savers Exchange, High Ground Gardens, Miss Penn's Mountain Seeds, and Hawthorn Farm Organic Seeds. Check http://Lofthouse.com for additional sellers.

Made in the USA
Las Vegas, NV
04 January 2022